Your Boss Era

Your Boss Era
Become the Manager Everyone Wants to Work For

Heather Elkington

EBURY EDGE

UK | USA | Canada | Ireland | Australia
India | New Zealand | South Africa

Ebury Edge is part of the Penguin Random House group of companies
whose addresses can be found at global.penguinrandomhouse.com

Penguin Random House UK
One Embassy Gardens, 8 Viaduct Gardens, London SW11 7BW

penguin.co.uk
global.penguinrandomhouse.com

Penguin
Random House
UK

First published by Ebury Edge in 2025
1

Typeset in 11.5/16.5pt Palatino Nova Pro by Six Red Marbles UK, Thetford, Norfolk
Printed and bound in India by Manipal Technologies Limited

The authorised representative in the EEA is Penguin Random House Ireland,
Morrison Chambers, 32 Nassau Street, Dublin D02 YH68

A CIP catalogue record for this book is available from the British Library

ISBN 9781529146967

MIX
Paper | Supporting
responsible forestry
FSC® C018179

Penguin Random House is committed to a sustainable future
for our business, our readers and our planet. This book is made
from Forest Stewardship Council® certified paper.

To Mum and Dad
Because your borderline delusional levels of optimism
about the world made me believe I could achieve literally
anything . . . and, somehow, you were right.

Contents

Introduction

Hi, I'm Heather. I used to think a Business Management degree would prepare me for leadership; that, by the time I walked out of university, I'd have it all figured out – I'd be confident, competent and ready to build a great career. Instead, I walked into my first management role feeling like an imposter.

I had spent three years sitting in lecture halls revising theories about what made a 'good manager'. I had memorised models, written essays on outdated case studies and could explain the difference between transformational and transactional leadership in an exam. But when I stepped into my first real leadership role, none of it prepared me for what actually mattered.

Nothing I learned at university taught me how to have a difficult conversation with an underperforming employee; how to balance being respected and being liked; or how to make decisions when there wasn't a 'right' answer, only a messy, uncertain one.

And yet, despite feeling wildly unprepared, I kept moving forward. I took the promotions, the pay rises, the next 'step up'. By 26, I had worked my way from assistant manager of a small team at Harrods to director of operations in a FTSE 100 subsidiary, leading five different teams.

I should have felt like a leader.

Instead, every decision I made felt like a test I wasn't qualified to take. Imposter syndrome sat in every meeting room with me, whispering that, one day, someone would figure out that I had no idea what I was doing. I was constantly looking over my shoulder, waiting for the moment I'd be 'found out'.

So, I did what I thought I was supposed to do. I worked harder. I took on more. I said yes to everything. I told myself that, when I hit the next milestone – when I got the next pay rise, the next title, the next big win – I would finally feel like I'd *made it*. I would finally *arrive* at the version of myself who had it all figured out.

But that moment never came.

Then, when I hit 27, something changed.

The Shift

At that point, my career was objectively successful. I was earning a six-figure salary with even bigger bonuses. I had built teams, scaled companies and even played a big role in exiting a business for eight figures. But none of those things were the reason I finally felt different.

For the first time in my life, I wasn't just 'surviving' my job. I wasn't working to prove something. I wasn't chasing the next title to quieten the voice in my head telling me I wasn't good enough. I actually *liked* being at work.

And not in the way I had before – where work was a game of achievement, a ladder I was trying to climb. I liked my job in a way that felt *healthy*. It added to my life instead of draining it.

My life outside of work was different, too. My circle was smaller – I had fewer friends than I used to, but the ones

I had were solid. After years of rocky relationships, I was finally in one that felt stable and real. I wasn't burning myself out trying to keep up with everyone else. I had created a life that actually felt good, instead of one that just looked good on the surface.

And that's when I realised: I was in *my* Boss Era.

What 'Your Boss Era' Actually Means

Your Boss Era isn't about promotions, pay rises or external validation (although that is some of the fun stuff you'll pick up along the way too). It's not about faking confidence until you believe it. And it's definitely not about working yourself into the ground to prove your worth.

As we move into our Boss Era, we step into a version of ourselves that is clear, capable and in control – of both your management career and also of your life.

It's about finding a rhythm that works for you – where work is something that fulfils you, not something you have to recover from every week.

It's about *finally* realising that being great at your job doesn't mean never struggling. That confidence isn't the absence of doubt. That leadership isn't about knowing everything – it's about showing up, having the courage to make the call and being okay when things don't always go as planned.

I wrote this book because I wish I'd had it when I started managing people. I spent years feeling like I was failing at leadership, even when I was getting results. I had to piece together my own blueprint through trial and error, through journaling, and through realising (often the hard way) what actually works.

And now, after thousands of hours spent managing teams, coaching leaders and testing these ideas in the real world, I've distilled everything I've learned into this book.

The 16 Rules

Leadership isn't something you're naturally either good at or bad at. It's not something you're born with. It's a clear set of *rules* – and, like any skill, they can be learned, practised and refined.

This book lays out 16 of the most important rules I've used to build high-performing teams and create impact, all while actually *enjoying* my job.

These aren't outdated corporate clichés or textbook theories. In fact, they go against almost everything I learned in my Business Management degree. They're practical, tested and designed for *real* workplaces – the kind with difficult personalities, shifting priorities and actual human dynamics.

Most leadership books are written from the perspective of someone reflecting from the top, from a senior position two decades later, full of wisdom but detached from the reality of what it takes to get started and from modern workplaces.

This book is different. I'm right here with you – just a step ahead in the leadership journey, reaching back to share what I've learned. I'm still figuring things out too, as I build another team from the ground up.

This book is written for *right now*. For managers stepping into leadership today, trying to navigate the complexity of managing people, while also trying to figure themselves out.

If that's you, you're in the right place.

HOW TO READ THIS BOOK

Your Boss Era is split into 16 chapters, and those 16 chapters are organised into two parts:

1. **People:** *Mastering the mindset*

2. **Systems:** *Mastering the mechanics*

Don't rush this book. There's a lot to learn and do. I'd rather you read one chapter each week, and commit to the actions as we go. Each chapter will only take you about 20 minutes to read, but months of commitment to master it.

Let's get started.

Part 1

People: Mastering the Mindset

Part 1

People: Mastering the Mindset

Leadership has had a bit of a facelift in recent years. While we traditionally valued authority, dominance and technical expertise in our business leaders, we now, thankfully, also recognise that leadership is about something far more human. People skills aren't just trendy buzzwords – they're the foundation of modern leadership. In fact, they'll shape your career in ways you might not expect, from the success of your hiring practice and how your company grows, to the legacy you leave behind.

Leadership hasn't always looked like this. For decades, it was about being decisive, results-driven and firmly in control. Success was measured by numbers: hitting targets, boosting productivity and maximising profits. People were seen as numbers on a spreadsheet to manage as efficiently as possible, rather than individuals to empower. That approach got results back then, but today's workplace has changed dramatically.

People now expect more from their leaders. They want to feel valued and heard. Hybrid work is here to stay, teams are more diverse, mental health and well-being have moved to the forefront of our workforce's minds, and leaders must rise to meet these challenges by showing up entirely differently.

A recent study by the University of Sunderland highlights that 85 per cent of job success stems from strong people skills, while only 15 per cent depends on technical abilities. This shift reflects the growing recognition that interpersonal abilities are essential for effective leadership and team collaboration, a trend that is compounded by a more diverse and globally dispersed workforce.

Take Jacinda Ardern, the former prime minister of New Zealand. She redefined leadership by leading with empathy and compassion. In response to the Christchurch mosque shootings in 2019, her approach wasn't cold or bureaucratic. It was deeply human. She stood in solidarity with the Muslim community, wearing a hijab and providing space for grief and healing. Her leadership wasn't about wielding power, but about making people feel seen, heard and supported. And it worked. Her ability to connect emotionally made New Zealand's response to the crisis one of the most praised in recent history. She proved that true leadership doesn't come from having all the answers, but from empathy, trust and vulnerability.

That's the power of people skills. They transform a manager into a great leader. Emotional intelligence (EI), adaptability, empathy and conflict resolution are essential. If you want to build strong teams, make a lasting impact and thrive as a leader, you need to prioritise these skills.

Many people assume that people skills are innate – something you're either born with or not. But that's far from the truth. Skills like courage, empathy and EI aren't fixed traits; they're abilities that can be developed with practice. Courage, for example, isn't about grand, heroic acts. It's about small moments of bravery, repeated over time, that shape you into a more confident and capable leader. The same applies to empathy, EI and the ability to inspire. These aren't mysterious gifts reserved for the naturally charismatic – they're skills anyone can develop with effort and intention.

What Are People Skills?

The *Cambridge Dictionary* defines people skills as 'the ability to deal with other people in a friendly and effective way'. In simpler terms, they're the human side of leadership, the skills that help you build trust, communicate effectively and handle challenges with empathy and EI.

Unlike technical skills (like coding, accounting or data analysis), people skills focus on how you approach situations and relationships. They include your strategic thinking, communication, conflict resolution and adaptability, among others.

These skills empower leaders to build trust, resolve conflicts and create an inclusive, thriving work environment. They're the foundation upon which technical expertise can be fully leveraged.

Consider this: a technically brilliant leader who lacks empathy or EI might achieve short-term success, but risks burning out their team and damaging morale. Without strong people skills, you can unintentionally stall progress and erode workplace culture.

The best leaders know how to inspire, connect and cultivate a culture where everyone feels valued. In this section, we'll explore the nine fundamental people skills you need to step into Your Boss Era – from earning respect and building trust to mastering high-level EI.

Let's dive in.

OUR BOSS ZINA

Rule #1

Own Your Emotions (or They'll Own You)

There's one moment from my early days in leadership that still makes me cringe. It was a fast-paced morning working at the start-up where I was leading a small (but mighty) team. We'd just launched a new product feature that, while innovative, was proving confusing for our users and caused a spike in support queries.

One client, in particular, was livid. They'd sent several emails – angry, urgent, desperate for help – but, in an unfortunate mix of events, they'd been emailing the wrong department, and their messages had slipped through the cracks. When they finally did get a response, it wasn't from the right team and offered no useful solutions.

By the time the complaint landed on my desk, the client was beyond annoyed. Although they'd sent the email to the wrong place, it didn't matter, their frustration was entirely justified. We should have handled it better and the fault was clearly ours. But somewhere between my rising stress levels and my emotional immaturity as a leader, I couldn't see it for what it was. Instead of recognising the situation objectively, I let my emotions cloud my judgement and reacted defensively. I let my emotions own me.

I still remember the moment I picked up the phone. I could feel my shoulders tense the second the client started talking, with the open-plan office quietening as people waited to see how I'd react. The client's frustration was spilling out in a torrent of blame, and I felt it all landing on *me*.

That was the trigger.

I felt a mix of embarrassment that this had slipped through the cracks, defensiveness over the team's processes and even some anger at the client for not following the 'right' steps.

Instead of pausing to get a grip on what I was feeling, I let those emotions take the wheel. My reaction was impulsive and stubborn – I told the client that if they'd emailed the right inbox from the start, they wouldn't be in this mess. No accountability was taken. Not my finest hour.

Only with hindsight did I see that that response didn't just make things worse with the client, it had a ripple effect across the business. The client left, frustrated with how we'd handled things, and they didn't leave quietly. They posted a scathing review online, criticising our service and warning others not to work with us.

And my team? They saw my reaction loud and clear. By shifting the blame on to the client, I unintentionally gave them permission to do the same. Over the next few months, I started to see glimpses of blame culture seeping through the cracks. When things went wrong, fingers were pointed outwards instead of inwards.

It wasn't long before the blame culture became glaringly obvious. Missed deadlines? Blamed on other departments. Poor customer feedback? Brushed off as 'difficult' clients. There was a pattern forming: no accountability, no ownership. Problems and mistakes weren't seen as opportunities to learn, they were just hot potatoes to be passed on to someone else.

And I knew deep down that I had participated in building this no-accountability culture. Your team do not do as you say, they do as you do.

I doubt the situation with that particular client was the sole catalyst for this culture to take hold. These things rarely come down to just one moment. But that call sticks in my mind so clearly because it was a turning point for me. A moment when I *could* have modelled accountability. And instead I did the opposite.

It was a stark reminder that how you choose to respond in those emotional, high-pressure moments doesn't just impact one situation – it shapes your team's behaviours, too. I could've de-escalated the situation, kept the client's trust and set a better example for my team.

It took me a while to see that, but, once I did, it became clear that I had to change how I led. If I wanted my team to take accountability and handle conflict well, I had to start by managing my own emotional reactions. What I *should* have done was paused, taken a second to acknowledge that I was feeling defensive and frustrated, and then responded with empathy and accountability.

And that moment became one of the most valuable lessons of my leadership journey: there's power in the pause.

The best leaders understand that between a trigger and a response, there's a critical moment – a pause – where we get to choose how to react. It's in that pause where real leadership can shine through.

What we're really talking about here is EI, or emotional intelligence: the ability to recognise and manage your own emotions while navigating the emotions of others. And it's no small thing. A comprehensive study by TalentSmartEQ examined the role of EI in job performance across various industries and roles. The research assessed participants on key EI competencies, and the findings revealed that EI accounts for 58 per cent of success in all job types, making it a critical factor in leadership effectiveness. Additionally, the study found that individuals with high EI earn an average of $29,000 more annually than their lower-EI counterparts, highlighting the financial benefits associated with strong EI.

This isn't just about staying calm for the sake of it or ignoring how we feel. It's about understanding how your emotional responses impact those around you – and learning how to channel those emotions to drive better outcomes for your team. It's about owning your emotions (before they own you).

Get the Emotional Advantage

In my own Boss Era, one of the biggest turning points was becoming super aware of my emotions and understanding that managing them is key to becoming a true leader. We should never be bottling them up or pretending they don't exist, but instead becoming aware of them, and using them to our advantage.

Emotions drive our behaviour. When we don't recognise our emotional triggers and manage our reactions, we risk creating toxic environments where fear, blame and frustration take over. Snap decisions made in anger or frustration lead to poor communication, defensive team members and mistrust. Over time, this erodes team morale and can even result in a blame culture – just as I experienced in my early days as a manager.

Letting emotions take control in the workplace often means leaders react impulsively rather than respond thoughtfully. Reacting before *the pause* can make a leader appear inconsistent, irrational or even unapproachable, which makes it difficult for their team to trust or follow them. It impacts everything from how decisions are made and how conflicts are handled, to how performance feedback is given. As a result, teams may avoid accountability, dread difficult conversations and lose motivation to push for better results.

By contrast, leaders with EI know how to separate their immediate feelings from the long-term outcomes they want to achieve. They understand that pausing to manage their emotions in the moment creates a more thoughtful, consistent approach that inspires trust and stability in their team.

It's all about steering clear of those impulsive reactions (just like the one I had with the angry client).

I wanted to kick off this book with EI because, as managers, we are in the business of dealing with people. How successful we are in our role is entirely dependent on how well we can manage a group of human beings – all with different personalities, values and emotional responses. Emotions are woven into every meeting, decision and conversation. To lead effectively, we need to recognise them, understand their impact and learn to manage them.

EI needs to be woven into how we lead until it becomes second nature. But do not fear, it is a skill like any other that can be learned, practised and eventually mastered.

The EI Framework

At its core, EI is about managing the space between a trigger (an event or situation that provokes an emotional reaction) and your response. That space, however small, is where true leadership shines. It's in that moment of pause that you choose whether to react impulsively or respond thoughtfully.

Now that we've established the importance of the trigger–response dynamic, let's dive into a well-known framework for understanding EI in leadership. Daniel Goleman, a psychologist and author, is widely credited with bringing the concept of EI into the mainstream with his groundbreaking work in the mid-1990s.

In 1995, Goleman published his bestselling book, *Emotional Intelligence: Why it can matter more than IQ*, which was based on earlier research by psychologists Peter Salovey and John Mayer. Goleman took their academic theory and made it accessible to a wider audience, particularly in the workplace. His book highlighted that EI – qualities like self-awareness, empathy and self-regulation – was often a better predictor of success than traditional measures like IQ.

Goleman's book revolutionised how we think about leadership. In 1998, he published an influential article in *Harvard Business Review* titled 'What makes a leader?', where he argued that EI is the single biggest factor in distinguishing great managers from average ones. His research found that 90 per cent of top-performing managers have high EI, and that it plays a critical role in creating trust, team cohesion and improving overall organisational performance.

Today, Goleman's framework for EI is still widely used in leadership development. It includes five key components which we will explore in detail and I'll provide practical steps to help you apply them in your leadership journey.

The five components are:

1. Self-awareness

2. Self-regulation

3. Motivation

4. Empathy

5. Social skills

1. SELF-AWARENESS: THE FOUNDATION OF EI

Self-awareness is where EI starts. It's about **understanding your own emotions**, recognising how they influence your thoughts and behaviours, and being honest with yourself about your strengths and weaknesses.

Without self-awareness, emotions can drive your behaviour in ways you don't even realise. Think about a time when you snapped at someone after a stressful meeting or felt defensive when your ideas were challenged. If you're unaware of your emotional triggers, those reactions can happen on autopilot – and they rarely lead to the best outcomes.

Imagine you're in a team meeting, and someone criticises your idea. Your first reaction might be to feel **defensive** or **irritated**. But if you're self-aware, you can catch those feelings as they come up and take a moment to reflect. You might realise that your response isn't about the feedback itself, but rather about a **fear of failure** or **insecurity** you're carrying.

Recognising that emotional trigger allows you to manage your reaction – perhaps by calmly asking for feedback to improve your idea, rather than shutting down or getting defensive.

In practice, this looks like:

- **Pausing before reacting.** When you feel frustration or defensiveness bubbling up, take a moment to ask yourself: *Why am I feeling this way? What's really triggering me?*

- **Tracking emotional patterns.** Start keeping a journal or making mental notes of situations that trigger strong emotional reactions. Are there patterns? Are there certain people or scenarios that always cause frustration or insecurity?

- **Seeking feedback.** Self-awareness isn't built only on internal reflections – it's also how you're perceived by others. Regularly ask your team or peers for feedback on how you show up as a leader. Do your actions align with your values?

- **Recognising strengths and weaknesses.** Self-awareness means acknowledging what you do well, but also being honest about where you aren't the strongest. Are you quick to dismiss ideas that aren't your own? Do you struggle to listen when under pressure?

Becoming emotionally aware is about recognising emotions as they arise and understanding where they're coming from. The more self-aware you are, the better equipped you'll be to make thoughtful decisions and handle difficult situations with clarity and composure.

2. SELF-REGULATION: THE POWER OF CONTROL

Once you've acknowledged the part emotions play in your reactions, the next step is learning how to manage those emotions in real time. This is where self-regulation comes in. Self-regulation is the ability to control your emotional impulses and respond in a way that aligns with your values and long-term goals, rather than letting your emotions dictate your behaviour.

In leadership, self-regulation is the difference between reacting impulsively and responding thoughtfully. We're not trying to suppress our emotions or pretend they don't exist. We can instead recognise them, pause and choose a response that serves the situation rather than escalates it.

Self-regulation is what keeps leaders calm under pressure, even in high-stakes situations. It's about making sure that short-term emotions don't derail long-term objectives. A manager who can stay composed, even in challenging moments, earns trust and respect.

At its core, self-regulation is about taking control of that trigger–response gap. It's about expressing your emotions, but in the right way, at the right time and for the right purpose.

In practice, self-regulation looks like:

- **Holding back from sending an email when you're angry** and revisiting it later.

- **Choosing your words carefully in high-stakes conversations.** For instance, removing overly emotive language and avoiding blame. Instead, focus on using neutral, fact-based terms that promote collaboration and clarity.

- **Staying calm in meetings where things don't go as planned.** De-escalate tensions by acknowledging frustrations and then guide the team back to the issues at hand. When challenges arise, pause, take a breath and invite your team to refocus on solutions by asking clarifying questions such as, 'What do we need to do next to overcome this setback?'

Self-regulation is a powerful skill that separates good leaders from great ones. The ability to stay **calm, collected and intentional** (even when emotions are running high) is what sets the tone for your team and shows them how to handle challenges effectively. Ask yourself: *What's the outcome I want from this conversation?* Then choose your response accordingly. It sounds simple, but it's incredibly powerful in practice.

3. MOTIVATION: KEEPING THINGS MOVING FORWARD

As a leader, your emotional state influences your team more than you realise. When you're driven and energised, your team feel that. But if you're demotivated, stressed or emotionally disengaged, that also spreads quickly. Your motivation (or lack of it) sets the emotional tone for your team.

Motivated leaders create emotionally engaged teams. According to Gallup's 2024 State of the Global Workplace Report, managers are responsible for an astonishing 70 per cent of the variation in team engagement. The report highlights that a leader's motivation and behaviours directly impact how engaged their team feels at work. In other words, a leader who understands their own emotional drivers and stays connected to their purpose is far more likely to inspire resilience, commitment and drive within their team.

In practice, motivation looks like:

- **Connecting to your 'why'.** When work feels overwhelming, remind yourself why you're doing it. Is it to help your team grow? To make an impact in your industry? Write down your values and revisit them regularly to stay emotionally aligned with your purpose.

  Now share your 'why' with your team. Motivation is contagious. Be transparent with your team about what drives you, whether it's making an impact, solving complex problems or helping them succeed. When your team understands your purpose, they're more likely to connect with their own.

- **Reframing challenges.** When faced with setbacks, pause and ask yourself: *What can I learn from this?* Instead of reacting emotionally to failure, look for opportunities to grow or improve.

- **Recognising emotional burnout.** Motivation is never about pushing through at all costs. It's about recognising when you need to pause and recharge. EI means knowing when to pull back so you can sustain your drive in the long term.

- **Celebrating small wins.** Motivation can wane when progress feels slow. To combat this, take time to recognise small achievements – both yours and your team's. This keeps emotional energy high and reinforces a positive mindset.

- **Checking in with your emotions.** Regularly ask yourself: *What emotions am I bringing into my work today? How are they impacting my motivation?* Identifying emotional

patterns can help you manage dips in motivation before
they affect your performance.

- **Modelling resilience.** When things go wrong, your team
  looks to you for how to react. If you stay calm, emotionally
  grounded and focused on solutions, you'll inspire your
  team to do the same.

Motivation, at its core, is about managing the emotional ups
and downs of leadership. It's about recognising when emotions are helping or hindering your progress, then using
that awareness to keep yourself and your team emotionally
engaged and committed to the bigger picture.

4. EMPATHY: THE HEART OF EMOTIONS IN LEADERSHIP

Empathy is the ability to truly understand and share the feelings of others. It's about putting yourself in someone else's
shoes and seeing things from their perspective. In leadership, empathy comes easier to some than others, but it's
essential for building trust and creating a supportive team
environment.

When Satya Nadella took over as CEO of Microsoft in
2014, the company was facing significant challenges, including a broken culture where many employees felt entitled and
disconnected. Nadella knew that to turn the company around,
he needed to reconnect with the people within it. Instead of
focusing solely on strategies and numbers, he made empathy
a big part of his leadership approach.

Satya Nadella encouraged open dialogue and genuinely
listened to employees at all levels of the company. One of
his first steps was to launch a series of 'CEO Connection'

meetings, where employees were invited to share their thoughts and ideas directly with him. He also implemented regular town hall meetings where employees could ask questions openly, creating a direct line of communication between leadership and the wider team.

Beyond meetings, Nadella prioritised ongoing feedback loops, introducing new tools and processes to ensure employees felt heard. He promoted growth mindset principles across the company, encouraging employees to see challenges as opportunities to learn rather than failures. Under his leadership, performance reviews shifted to focus more on collaboration, learning and impact rather than just individual results – reinforcing the importance of listening, improving and working together.

This approach had a profound impact. By showing that he valued the perspectives and well-being of his employees and making practical changes to ensure those values were reflected in everyday practices, Nadella rebuilt trust and morale within the organisation. This, in turn, sparked a culture of collaboration and innovation, playing a critical role in Microsoft's resurgence as a tech leader.

We can develop our empathy for our teams daily by:

- **Holding regular open forums for feedback.** Create safe spaces – like team check-ins or anonymous feedback tools – where employees can share concerns, ideas and frustrations without fear of judgement.

- **Actively listening and responding.** When someone shares feedback, don't just nod along. Ask follow-up questions, acknowledge their feelings and take actionable steps to address their concerns. People need to feel heard *and* see results. (See page 225 for some more tips to improve your listening.)

- **Creating ongoing feedback loops.** Never let feedback be a once-a-year event. We will learn much more about this in Rules #10 and #11, but to get started, commit to building continuous feedback into your team, keeping communication open and addressing issues before they escalate.

5. SOCIAL SKILLS: THE ART OF INFLUENCE

This is the last step in the EI framework, but one never to overlook. When we talk about **social skills** in the context of EI, we're not just talking about being friendly or sociable. Strong social skills are about understanding and managing the emotional dynamics within your team to build relationships and influence outcomes.

Leaders often fall into the trap of focusing on themselves – their targets, their ideas and their vision. But great leaders understand that leadership isn't about you; it's about the people you serve. To influence, inspire and motivate a team, you first need to build your social skills by showing genuine interest in your people – not just in what they can do for you, but in who they are, what they value and what drives them.

'You can make more friends in two months by becoming interested in other people than you can in two years by trying to get other people interested in you.' This quote from Dale Carnegie's *How to Win Friends and Influence People* shows us the importance of genuine interest in others as a cornerstone of flexing our social skills muscle.

Think of it this way: your social skills are the bridge between your EI and your leadership effectiveness. You can be self-aware, manage your emotions and feel empathy, but if you don't know how to communicate and connect with people, your impact as a leader will be limited.

In practice, this looks like:

- **Practising active listening.** Next time you're in a meeting, focus entirely on the person speaking. Put away distractions, make eye contact and ask clarifying questions. Instead of thinking about your next response, listen in order to understand their point of view. This builds trust and shows your team that their opinions matter. (There are more tips on active listening on page 225.)

- **Being genuinely interested.** Great leaders aim to be interested, not interesting.

- **Adapting your communication style to fit different personalities.** Not everyone on your team communicates in the same way. Some people prefer direct, to-the-point conversations, while others need more context and reassurance. Pay attention to how each team member responds in different situations and adjust your approach accordingly.

Social skills are the tools you use to build trust, navigate difficult conversations and inspire your team to take action. Without them, even the best intentions and strategies can fall flat.

What makes social skills so powerful is their ability to amplify all the other components of EI. Self-awareness, self-regulation, motivation and empathy all come to life through your interactions with others. It's through your words, actions and connections that your leadership truly takes shape.

Strong social skills aren't about being naturally charismatic or outgoing. They're about being intentional: actively listening, adapting your communication style and showing a genuine interest in your team.

The Emotional Edge

As we've seen, EI is the foundation of effective management. It's not pretending emotions don't exist or trying to push them aside. It's recognising how they show up in your decisions and interactions, managing them with intention and using them to build trust, strengthen relationships and move your team in the right direction.

Each of the five key components we've explored in this chapter is essential for building emotional maturity as a manager and creating a team environment where people feel valued, respected and inspired to grow.

But I want to take this idea of EI just one small step further. Some of the emotions we have branded as 'weak' or 'bad', like nervousness, fear or anger, aren't actually bad at all. They aren't to be avoided – they're simply signals. The way we interpret and manage those emotions can completely change how we show up as leaders.

Let me take you back to when I was fresh out of university and facing my first big interview. After weeks of furiously applying, I'd finally secured an interview with a small team working inside Harrods. I was ecstatic. But as the interview date approached, my excitement turned to doubt, worry and fear. The night before, I was in such a state that I was considering

Great leaders aim to be interested, not interesting.

cancelling the whole thing when my dad, with his calm wisdom, said something that changed everything for me: 'Heather, nerves build character. You're supposed to be nervous.'

My nerves weren't a sign that I wasn't capable – they were a sign that I was about to step into something challenging and meaningful. I reframed my nervousness as excitement, and that shift in mindset over the years has really changed everything for me. Instead of being paralysed by fear, I often feel energised and ready to face the challenge ahead. Nerves don't have to stifle us; they can be a sign that we're moving in the right direction. It's a signal that we're doing something important, something we care deeply about. It shows investment, commitment and growth.

As a leader, you'll encounter these kinds of emotions in yourself and in your team – before big presentations, during difficult conversations or when stepping into new roles. Your job isn't to eliminate those feelings, but to help yourself and others navigate through them. For example, if your team is about to pitch to a major client, I recommend addressing the nervousness openly. By acknowledging that anxiety is natural and beneficial, you create an environment where team members feel safe to share their concerns and support one another. This approach not only validates their emotions, but also helps to channel that nervous energy into focus and drive, ultimately strengthening your collective performance.

The true power of EI lies in how it transforms the actions taken by both you and your team. It helps you stay composed in tough situations and creates a culture where people feel safe to step outside their comfort zones. Managers who begin to master EI build resilient teams that thrive under pressure, adapt to change and push through challenges with clarity and confidence.

The one key to unlocking this advantage is recognising that emotions aren't the enemy – they're actually our secret weapon. All you need to do is commit to understanding and managing them, and you'll be well on your way to managing with powerful impact.

And that brings us to the next crucial lesson – because emotional intelligence isn't about being 'nice' all the time.

Stop Being Nice, Start Being Kind

In the previous chapter, we explored the role emotions play in management and how understanding them helps us build trust. But what happens when that trust is tested? When you have to deliver hard truths or hold someone accountable without damaging relationships? It's time to find that sweet spot where you can balance empathy with honesty, and compassion with candour.

Let's go back to 2021. I was right in the middle of one of the biggest moments of my career – the sale of our small start-up, GoProposal, to a huge corporate, Sage. This wasn't just another business deal – it was the culmination of years of hard work, dedication, growth and a huge vision finally coming to life. The stakes were high, with tens of millions of pounds on the line, and a lot of it came down to me and how I presented the company.

I was nervous, but I'd practised endlessly, preparing myself for the presentations and dinners. I knew that how I presented – how I communicated – would play a massive role in whether we secured the deal. So, I put everything into it. And around came one of the final presentations. Afterwards, we wrapped things up and I went out for a fancy dinner with the founder of GoProposal and a few of the Sage executives. After dinner, the founder of GoProposal pulled me aside. He looked me in the eyes and said, 'Heather, I need to give you some feedback: you talk too fast and I can't understand what you're saying.'

At first, I was taken aback. I felt hurt, annoyed and, honestly, a bit angry. How could he say that after all the effort I'd put in? And right now? It absolutely was not the 'nice' thing to say there and then.

So I went back to my hotel, and because I had started working on my emotional intelligence, instead of focusing too much on being defensive, I sat and pondered his words. Then, the next morning, instead of wallowing in self-pity, I decided to do something about it. I started reading, listening to podcasts and learning everything I could about effective communication. I wanted to understand *why* I was talking so fast and how I could fix it. What I discovered was eye-opening: my fast talking was a symptom of my insecurity. I was rushing through my words because, deep down, I wasn't confident in my voice.

That feedback marked a turning point. It set me on a path of self-improvement that eventually led me to become a TEDx speaker, addressing thousands of people and working with some of the biggest companies out there. I wouldn't have achieved any of that if I hadn't received that difficult feedback.

If he wanted to be 'nice', he would have said nothing. It would have spared my feelings in the moment, sure. But being kind and telling me the uncomfortable truth was the best thing he could have done for me in that moment. He wasn't trying to put me down; he was trying to help me grow. It wasn't about being nice; it was about being honest. And that honesty, though hard to swallow at the time, was a real act of kindness.

Let's look at the difference between being nice and being kind . . .

Being Nice Versus Being Kind

Nice / *adjective*
Giving pleasure or satisfaction.

The definition of being nice is to give pleasure or be pleasant. Just let those words sit for a second. Being kind on the other hand . . .

Kind / *adjective*
Having or showing a friendly, generous and considerate nature.

Being kind is to be generous or considerate. Which one would you rather be? Someone who gives pleasure to others? Or someone who is considerate?

Knowing and understanding the difference between being nice and being kind is essential when you're in a leadership role. Being nice is all about keeping the peace, avoiding conflict and making sure everyone feels good in the moment. It's about being agreeable and pleasant, even if it means hiding your true feelings or avoiding the hard conversations.

Being kind, however, is about doing what's right, even when it's difficult. It's about caring enough to be honest, to challenge someone when necessary and to help them grow.

In managers, I have observed niceness showing up in three ways:

1. Sugar-coated feedback.

2. Avoiding tough conversations.

3. Saying yes to every request just to keep people happy.

While this approach might seem like it keeps the peace and wins you short-term validation, it is a form of false harmony, and it comes at a much bigger cost: you lose long-term respect.

Let's focus on the first point: sugar-coated feedback. Imagine you have a team member who's underperforming. They're missing deadlines or their work isn't meeting the standard you expect. You know you need to give them feedback, but you don't want to come across as too harsh. So, you use what's often called the 'sh*t sandwich' method.

You start with something positive, like, 'Hey, I just want to say you've been doing a great job on X . . .' Then, you lightly touch on the issue: 'It would be great if you could be a bit more mindful of deadlines . . .' And you finish with another positive: 'But overall, you're doing a great job and I'm really happy with your work!'

At first glance, this seems like a polite and supportive way to give feedback. But here's what actually happens . . .

Your team member hears the positives loud and clear – and the core feedback, the part they really need to hear, gets diluted. They leave the conversation feeling like everything is mostly fine. Nothing changes. Then, before you know it, frustration builds up, and their performance and your relationship start to suffer. All because you were 'nice'. It was easier for you, sure, but you've stolen a learning and growth opportunity from your team member.

The kind thing to do in this situation isn't to sugar-coat the feedback to spare their feelings. It's to deliver the feedback

35

clearly, directly and with respect, so they understand exactly what needs to change. A direct approach could sound like this:

> I need to talk to you about the deadlines we've been missing. It's becoming a problem, and I want to help you get ahead of it. Let's figure out what's going on and what we can do to improve.

Or:

> I've noticed that your recent work hasn't been meeting the standard we discussed. I want to make sure we address this now so you're set up to succeed moving forward.

Being direct doesn't mean being rude or harsh. It means being honest and clear. And, most importantly, it shows you care about the long-term growth of your team, rather than just their short-term satisfaction and comfort.

Being kind as a leader means valuing clarity over comfort. It's about creating a culture where people know exactly where they stand, rather than leaving them guessing. Your team will respect you more for being honest, even if it's uncomfortable at first, because they'll know you're invested in their success.

When we keep quiet about our concerns because we don't want to upset anyone, we miss out on the chance to steer the team in the right direction. We might end up going down a path we knew wasn't the best, only to face the fallout later. None of that is to say that praise isn't important. You want to focus on the good stuff and look for things to praise. Praise is an important part of showing appreciation and gratitude, important for any relationship to flourish. However, if you're using praise as nothing more than a criticism delivery platform, you're undervaluing praise and making your criticism unclear and unhelpful.

Another of the biggest 'nice' traps is feeling like you have to say yes to every request for help from your team. It might feel like the right thing to do – being there for them, being supportive – but what actually happens is that you lose focus on your own important work. You become a bottleneck, and your team becomes dependent on you to solve their problems, stifling their own growth. So, what's the kind way to respond when someone on your team asks for help that you *shouldn't* take on?

Let's say a team member comes to you with a question they could figure out themselves with a bit of effort. The nice response would be to immediately give them the answer, thinking you're saving them time. But the *kind* response would be to say something like:

I'm confident you've got this. Why don't you take a stab at it and come back to me if you hit a roadblock?

Or:

I can't take this on right now, but I'd love to see how you would solve it. Bring me your ideas, and we can chat through them together.

This way, you're showing support without taking the work on yourself. You're empowering your team to think independently and reinforcing that you trust their judgement. And that's what kindness looks like in leadership: building clarity, confidence and capability in your team – without carrying all the weight yourself.

Kindness also means empowering your team by giving them the space to solve their own problems. Instead of rushing in to save the day, step back and let them figure it out. This not only helps them develop their skills, but also encourages a sense of ownership and responsibility. Your team becomes more capable and resilient, and you avoid becoming the go-to fixer for every issue.

This sense of empowerment in your team doesn't come from being nice; it comes from being kind – by creating an environment where honesty, constructive criticism and autonomy are the norms. It also creates that magical concept, psychological safety – a culture where team members feel safe to take risks, make mistakes and learn from them without fear of punishment. There's much more on this in Rule #5, but psychological safety starts by giving your team the true freedom to solve their own challenges.

Kindness in Tough Conversations

Here's the thing about leadership that most people won't tell you: the hardest conversations, the ones where you have to put your niceness to the side, are the most important ones.

If niceness is all about avoiding discomfort and keeping things light in the short term, then kindness is about long-term growth. It's about being honest when it's hard. It's about building real respect through integrity and trust – *not* through being the manager who just wants everyone to like them. And that's where tough conversations come in.

We'll dive deeper into handling difficult conversations and navigating conflict in Rule #11, but for now, know this: real kindness isn't about avoiding discomfort – it's about facing it with honesty and care.

You can't lead a team without having tough conversations. They come up all the time: when someone isn't meeting expectations, when conflict bubbles up or when feedback needs to be given. Avoiding those moments might feel easier in the short term. We all love avoiding conflict. It's tempting to think, *I'll let it slide; I don't want to cause tension*. But that avoidance builds up over time. Missed deadlines, slipping standards, a general sense that *good enough* is the bar – and that's how you end up with a team that's stuck, disengaged or, worse, resentful.

Why? Because people notice when you don't say what needs to be said. Your high performers notice when under-performance in others is ignored. Your struggling team members notice in the long run when they're not given feedback that could actually help them improve. And, slowly, your team's culture starts to shift from one of accountability and growth . . . to one of avoidance and mediocrity. The very thing you were trying to avoid by being 'nice' ends up happening anyway. Only now, it's worse.

Tough conversations don't actually *create* conflict. The conflict already exists. The conversation is simply the next step to help *calling people up* to a higher standard. It's where we exercise kindness enough to say, 'I believe in you enough to have this conversation, because I know you're capable of more. I will put my fear of conflict aside, and have the courage to have this conversation with you.'

Kindness is saying what needs to be said, even when it's hard. It's choosing someone's growth over your own

39

short-term comfort. And that's the foundation of a high-performing, resilient and motivated team.

Because your team takes its cues from you, the way *you* show up sets the tone. When you embrace tough conversations, you create a team that won't stay silent when things aren't working, a team that trusts you to be honest with them, even when it's uncomfortable. And, in turn, they'll mirror that honesty back to you and each other.

I'm under no illusion that being the one to say the hard thing is easy.

Many managers struggle to give direct feedback, especially when they think it will be poorly received. And it's no wonder – being honest, particularly when the feedback might cause discomfort or conflict, is one of the hardest parts of leadership. It's human nature to want to avoid awkward moments. We don't want to hurt someone's feelings or be seen as difficult. But here's the truth: avoiding honesty doesn't protect your team – it holds them back.

Honesty saves everyone's time. It eliminates confusion, reduces frustration and prevents missed opportunities. When you're upfront about expectations, performance and decisions, your team knows where they stand. And when people know where they stand, trust grows. Trust is the foundation of every strong relationship – especially between a manager and their team.

But there is a fine line between honesty and *brutal* honesty . . . time to explore that now.

THE DARK SIDE OF 'KINDNESS'

There's a risk that some leaders take this advice too far and mistake honesty for bluntness. They think that telling it like it is, with no filter or empathy, is 'just being honest'. But there's a big difference between being honest and being hurtful.

Honesty without EI isn't kindness. It's simply cruelty dressed up as leadership. And here's the thing: most people who fall into this trap don't even realise they're doing it. They think they're being 'direct' or 'straight-talking', but what they're really doing is bulldozing through conversations with no regard for the other person's feelings, growth or experience. It's leadership at its laziest.

Anyone can point out what's wrong or deliver harsh truths. It takes no skill to say, 'This isn't good enough' or, 'You're not ready for this role.' The real skill is delivering the truth in a way that actually helps someone move forward. That's what separates great managers from abrasive ones.

Imagine you're managing someone who's struggling to meet the expectations of a big project. You could take the blunt approach and say, 'I don't think you're capable of leading this project.' It's honest, sure – but what does it achieve? The person leaves that conversation feeling defeated, embarrassed and likely frustrated. They're not any closer to improving or understanding where they went wrong. In fact, they're probably walking away wondering if they should start looking for a new job.

Now, compare that to a more thoughtful approach: 'Here's what I think you need to develop before you take on something at that level, and I'll support you to get there.' You've still delivered a difficult message, but you've done it in a way that opens the door to growth. Instead of shutting someone down, you've given them clarity on what they need to improve and, crucially, you've shown that you're willing to help them get there. That's leadership.

Here's another example. Let's say someone on your team

41

isn't pulling their weight. The blunt version of this conversation might be: 'You're not doing your job properly.' Again, it's honest. But what does that honesty do? It puts the other person on the defensive. They'll walk away feeling attacked, demoralised and probably annoyed at you for not offering any constructive advice.

A better version? 'I've noticed that some of your recent work isn't hitting the standard we agreed on. Let's talk about what's going on and figure out how we can get things back on track.' It's still honest. It's still direct. But it's also constructive. You're showing that you care enough to address the issue, and you're making it clear that you're willing to collaborate on a solution.

The reality is, how you say something is often more important than what you say.

Bluntness may feel effective in the moment, but it comes at a cost. Blunt honesty breaks trust. It makes people feel small. Your team will start avoiding you because they don't want to be on the receiving end of your feedback. Over time, it erodes psychological safety – the very thing that makes teams perform at their best.

On the flip side, thoughtful honesty builds trust. It makes your team feel supported, even when the conversation is difficult. It creates an environment where people aren't afraid to admit when they're struggling, because they know they'll be met with curiosity and support, not judgement or shame.

Let's call this the difference between feedback and fallout.

Blunt honesty causes fallout. It damages relationships and demoralises people. Thoughtful honesty is feedback – it builds people up, gives them clarity and helps them grow. It's what makes people walk out of a difficult conversation feeling like, 'Okay, that was hard to hear, but I know what I need to do now. And I know they're in my corner.' (Exactly how I felt after being told I spoke too fast.)

We are not sugar-coating things or dancing around the point. Being thoughtful doesn't mean being vague. It just means taking a moment to ask yourself, *What's the most helpful way I can say this? What is the kindest way I can say this? How do I deliver this feedback in a way that leaves this person feeling motivated to improve, not defeated?*

Here's a simple framework to keep in mind when delivering feedback:

1. **What's the issue?** Be specific about what isn't working.

2. **Why does it matter?** Connect it to a bigger picture – whether that's the team's success, their personal growth or the project's outcome.

3. **What's next?** Offer a path forward. What do they need to do to improve? And how will you support them?

So, instead of saying, 'This isn't good enough,' you say, 'This needs improvement. Here's what specifically needs to change, and here's how I can help.'

Instead of saying, 'You're not ready for this,' you say, 'Here's what I'd like to see from you before you take on a project at that level.'

Honesty that lifts people up is where the magic happens.

The other risk? Office politics.

There are times when the kindest thing to say isn't necessarily the most appropriate thing to say. Whether it's navigating senior stakeholders, dealing with sensitive company changes, or managing someone's departure, leadership isn't always black and white. We can't always be blurting out every truth in the moment. We need to deliver honesty with thoughtfulness and care.

Sometimes, you'll need to ask yourself: Is sharing this information helpful right now? Or is it self-serving? Will it cause unnecessary panic or confusion?

For example: when a project is delayed and you're in a meeting to discuss it, blunt honesty would look like: 'This project is going to fail because the timelines are unrealistic.' Instead, thoughtful honesty would be: 'I'm losing confidence in this project a little. Can we adjust our timeline to ensure the quality of this project meets expectations? Let's work together on a realistic plan to move forward.'

Good leaders don't avoid hard conversations. But *great* leaders know that honesty needs to be balanced with EI, empathy and timing. This is where judgement comes in. It's about knowing when to say something, how to say it and how much to share.

Honesty Saves Everyone's Time

Honesty is a critical part of being a successful manager. When leaders are upfront and honest with their team, they eliminate confusion, reduce frustration and avoid missed opportunities. This honesty builds trust, which is the foundation of any strong relationship. But it's not about saying *everything* that comes to mind in *every* situation. It's about using your judgement to know when honesty will help your team grow – and when it will just add noise.

So, stop being nice and start being kind today. It's a simple shift, but it can transform your leadership and your team's success. Make honesty and kindness your values, and you'll not only be a better leader, but you'll also create a work environment where everyone around you can thrive and grow from the feedback. Kindness is about being brave enough to be honest, even when it's uncomfortable. And it will set you head and shoulders above the rest of the leaders. It's a lesson I've learned the hard way, and I only hope it will be as impactful for you as it has been for me.

Once you embrace kindness over niceness, you unlock the next level of leadership – the ability to truly inspire and motivate others to reach new heights.

Leverage the Science of Inspiration and Motivation

When you think of someone truly inspiring, someone who can motivate others to do amazing things, who pops into your mind? Oprah Winfrey, whose resilience and influence have shaped generations, helping countless people believe in their own potential and embrace their stories? Nelson Mandela, a beacon of hope and justice, who united a divided nation and inspired millions to fight for equality and forgiveness? Or perhaps it's Bill Gates, not just for his groundbreaking role in revolutionising technology, but for empowering global communities to tackle pressing issues like poverty, disease and access to education through his philanthropy?

These figures might seem like giants, almost untouchable, far removed from the realities of your everyday work life. It's natural to wonder how you, reading this book right now, can ever hope to inspire others with that same level of greatness. But here's a little secret: inspiring others isn't a gift reserved for the great few. You can inspire your team too. Inspiration is a skill that can be learned and perfected, just like any other.

The truth is, none of these leaders was born knowing how to inspire and motivate. They developed the skill over time through deliberate effort, reflection and a commitment to growth. And if they could do it on a global scale, I knew I could find ways to bring those sparks into my team too.

But why should we even care about being an inspiring leader? For me, it's not about being an inspiring leader who is just admired – inspiring leaders who have the ability to motivate are the ones who get the results. A study by Bain & Company, which surveyed over 2,000 employees across different industries, found that people who feel inspired by their leaders are more than twice as productive as those who are just satisfied.

But let's talk about you for a second. Beyond the business benefits, being an inspiring leader can transform your own experience in your day-to-day work. Think about how rewarding it feels to know you've genuinely made a difference to someone's day, their career or even their life. Inspiring others brings so much more to our role – it can make the hard days feel worth it and the great days even better. When you inspire your team, you're building a legacy of impact that extends far beyond the tasks on your to-do list.

You don't need to build the next groundbreaking technology or revolutionise healthcare to earn the praise 'you're such an inspiration'. Day-to-day inspiration is simply about connecting our actions and those of others to a larger purpose. It's about showing your team how their work contributes to something far greater than just answering emails or managing projects. And, in this chapter, I'm going to tell you how you can be that person.

Being inspirational is showing your team the bigger picture and understanding what drives them on a personal level. In this sense, inspiration and motivation go hand in hand. In the next section, we're going to explore motivation: what it really means, why it matters and how understanding it can transform your ability to lead.

Where Does Motivation Come From?

Motivation comes in two main forms: intrinsic and extrinsic. Intrinsic motivation is driven by internal rewards – things like a sense of purpose, personal growth or joy in the task itself. Extrinsic motivation, on the other hand, comes from external rewards, such as completing tasks, hitting key performance indicators (KPIs) or earning recognition.

Research consistently shows that intrinsic motivation is far more effective in driving long-term, consistent behaviour. In fact, a study published in *Frontiers in Psychology* found that people with high intrinsic motivation are 45 per cent more likely to sustain their goals over time compared to those driven primarily by external rewards.

Let's break it down with a simple example. Imagine you set a goal to get a six-pack purely to look good on your summer holiday (extrinsic motivation). Chances are, once the holiday is over, or if the effort becomes too frustrating, you'll lose interest. Now, compare that to setting a goal to improve your mental health, feel stronger or build a better relationship with your body (intrinsic motivation). The second goal taps into deeper, more meaningful drivers, making it far easier to stay consistent, even when progress feels slow.

This difference is crucial for managers to understand. Helping your team connect their work to intrinsic motivators, like growth, purpose or personal satisfaction, can unlock a whole new level of engagement and performance.

For example, let's say your team is responsible for completing a large, tedious data analysis project. If the only motivator spoken about is meeting the deadline (an extrinsic reward), they might lose steam or disengage halfway through. But if you help them see the bigger picture – how their analysis will influence critical decisions, help the company achieve a meaningful goal or even build their skills for future career growth – you're tapping into an intrinsic motivation. By framing the work as purposeful and connected to their development, you'll create a more engaged, committed team that's willing to push through challenges.

When I was 18, I set a bold goal for myself: *own my own business and be a millionaire by 25*. At the time, this goal was driven purely by extrinsic motivation: the idea of wealth, status and unrealistic visions of what success should look like. I thought that reaching this milestone would validate my worth and show the world (and my parents) that I had 'made it' (yuck).

But, as my 25th birthday came and went, I was working in my 9–5 and actually really loving it. I loved how much I was learning and growing in my corporate role, so I took the pressure off myself a little and started questioning my true aspirations in life. Why wasn't I as motivated or driven to keep chasing that 'millionaire' pipe dream? Did I still want to become a business owner? I realised that by putting 'millionaire' first, I had been chasing a goal that, deep down, didn't resonate with what I truly wanted out of life.

It wasn't until I shifted my focus to my more intrinsic goals – like the freedom I wanted over my own time, the idea of working on projects I cared deeply about, to actually enjoy coming to work, to not have the 'Sunday scaries' and make a meaningful impact on the business and my team – that everything began to change for me. I realised that the passion for creating something that aligned with my values and allowed me to grow as a person was far more motivating than those external rewards I had been chasing.

This led me to create leadership principles that focused on collaboration, trust and autonomy. I started experimenting with giving my team the freedom to find their own solutions to problems, organise their workflows and contribute their ideas. I also worked on creating an environment where people felt genuinely supported and valued – not just as employees, but as individuals. These principles didn't just improve my team's performance, they also made me feel far more fulfilled in my role.

A study from McKinsey found that employees who are intrinsically motivated show 46 per cent higher levels of job satisfaction and 32 per cent greater commitment to their jobs. These employees are also less likely to experience burnout, making them more likely to stay with their employers for the long haul. We consistently find that intrinsic goals win out every single time.

For instance, the study highlighted that while extrinsic motivators like salary increases or bonuses can provide a short-term boost, they pale in comparison to the lasting impact of intrinsic drivers such as a sense of purpose or personal growth. One company cited in the study found that recognising employees for their contributions and connecting their work to meaningful outcomes – like how their efforts improved a client's life – led to a sustained increase in engagement and performance, far beyond what monetary incentives achieved.

Great managers leverage this psychological concept to inspire their teams daily. They ensure that their team's work is always connected to their intrinsic motivators, inspiring them to do their best work – whether it's for themselves, their clients or the broader impact their team is making on the world.

Simply put: neither you nor your team get out of bed excited to tick off tasks and write reports. We get out of bed excited when we know there's a bigger purpose driving our actions, and that we, as individuals, can genuinely contribute to that goal.

> Our passions are ignited when we set out to advance a cause greater than ourselves.
>
> Simon Sinek

Individual Motivators

Figuring out what really motivates your team involves a few simple steps that can help you tap into their personal values, passions and what genuinely drives them. Taking the time to understand what makes each person tick goes a little deeper than most team member–manager surface-level connections. But done well, it will be the foundation for a more inspired, aligned and motivated team.

We need to start by taking the time to get to know them. We'll dig a little deeper into the full '1-on-1 system' in Rule #10, but, for now, ask some questions that give them the space to open up. In a relaxed setting, I always encourage asking open-ended questions regularly, like:

- 'What parts of your work do you find the most rewarding?'
- 'What are you passionate about outside of work that you'd love to bring into your role?'
- 'What matters most to you, both at work and in life?'

When you start to hear and understand what drives people, over time, you'll be able to start matching tasks and projects to their strengths and interests, which not only keeps them engaged, but also boosts their performance. It also helps you give feedback and recognition in ways that actually resonate with them, building trust and respect.

Plus, knowing what someone values means you can spot potential challenges before they become full-blown issues. For example, if you learn that someone loves stability and clear processes, you'll realise that throwing last-minute deadlines or sudden changes their way might throw them off balance. So, instead, you can plan a little further ahead, give them a heads-up about what's coming or involve them in the planning so they feel more in control – staying one step ahead to avoid issues and showing your team that you've got their back.

As well as individual intrinsic motivators, it's just as important to connect individual motivations to the company's vision and mission, because when personal goals align with the organisation's purpose, it creates a sense of belonging and shared direction. People feel that their work matters – not just to them, but to the bigger picture. When everyone can see how what they're working on fits into the bigger picture, it gives their work more meaning and makes them more motivated to pull together towards the team's goals.

Team Motivators

While everyone has their own personal drivers, there's something powerful about tapping into what motivates the team as a whole. That's where your company's vision and/or mission statement comes in. If you've ever thought a mission statement was just words on a wall, you aren't alone. But a mission statement, used properly, should connect the team to shared purpose and something bigger. A mission statement should give your team a sense of direction and meaning beyond their day-to-day tasks. Take the following company mission statements for example:

- Patagonia: 'We're in business to save our home planet.'

- Tesla: 'To accelerate the world's transition to sustainable energy.'

- LinkedIn: 'To connect the world's professionals to make them more productive and successful.'

- Google: 'To organize the world's information and make it universally accessible and useful.'

If your team members chose to work for your company, there's a good chance they already believe in that vision or mission on some level. In fact, a recent LinkedIn study found that 68 per cent of professionals in Europe and 87 per cent in the US think it's important to work for companies that share their values. For younger generations like Gen Z and Millennials, it's even stronger: almost 90 per cent said they'd leave a job for one that better aligns with their values.

This tells us something simple but powerful about connecting your team's work to the company's bigger purpose: it is essential to leadership. When people feel their efforts contribute to something meaningful, they're more inspired, motivated and engaged.

So, whenever you're looking to rally your team, start with the company's mission. Ask yourself: how does this project tie into the impact we're all here to create? Then, bring that connection to life for your team. Whether it's through a shared goal, a reminder of the difference their work makes or celebrating milestones that align with the mission, linking what they do to the bigger picture makes all the difference.

Delegation with Purpose

Now it's time to put what we've learned into practice. I'm going to use some examples of a company vision statement, alongside my own intrinsic values, to show how we can motivate and inspire our team.

This is where delegation comes into play. For too long, managers have seen delegation as a way of just getting things off their plate. But, done well, delegation is about giving your team meaningful opportunities to contribute in ways that align with both their personal strengths and the organisation's goals. When you delegate effectively, you're not only freeing yourself to focus on higher-level responsibilities, you're also recognising the expertise within your team and showing them you trust their abilities.

Let's assume we are a technology company and I'm in your team. From everything we've just been through, here's what you need to know:

Company vision (the big-picture future the organisation aims to create):
'To create a world where every person has access to cutting-edge, user-friendly technology that enhances their daily life.'

Company mission (the roadmap for how it's going to get there):
'To design, manufacture and deliver innovative technology solutions that are accessible, reliable and tailored to meet the needs of our diverse customer base.'

Team member's intrinsic motivations:
Freedom of choice, gratitude, mental and physical health, and peace.

Now that you know these three things, you've got a powerful foundation to connect your team's tasks to something bigger to give them that spark of inspiration.

Instead of just assigning me a task without context, you can frame it in a way that ties my work to the bigger picture while respecting my intrinsic motivations. For instance, you might say:

This project's about making our tech more accessible for people who might not usually feel included in the tech world. (*Mission.*) I know you're great at coming

55

up with simple, clear solutions, so I'd love for you to take the lead on brainstorming ideas – feel free to structure your approach in whatever way that works best for you. (*Intrinsic motivations: freedom and gratitude.*) And if you need anything along the way, just give me a shout.

In this example, you're connecting the task to the company's mission of making technology accessible and inclusive, while also appealing to my values of freedom of choice and gratitude by letting me structure the work my way and showing trust in my abilities. By doing this, you're not just handing over a task, you're using delegation to inspire me with a sense of purpose and empowerment.

The next time you delegate a task, start by connecting it to something that resonates with your team member on a deeper level.

You might usually say:

Please run a report for me on our clients, with columns for their average monthly revenue, product usage and location. I need it by Friday.

You'll get: a report, with the requested information, by Friday. It's a straightforward task with a straightforward outcome – something that happens every day in the working world.

But what if you could motivate them by tying the task to their intrinsic values? Let's take the same example, but now you're thinking about their need for autonomy and creativity (freedom of choice), and how their work could contribute to something meaningful.

Instead, you might say:

Hey [team member], for this report, I'm looking for insights into how our top clients are engaging with our products – their average monthly revenue, product usage and location. I know how much you value having the freedom to approach tasks in your own way, so feel free to structure the report in a way that makes sense to you, as long as it includes those key data points. I trust your expertise to bring out something insightful.

The difference here? You're still providing clear expectations and outlining the specific information you need, but you're also giving them the space to approach the task creatively. This balance ensures you get the consistency and detail required while empowering them to take ownership of how they deliver the work.

If you're worried about misalignment or receiving something unexpected, use these simple delegation guidelines:

- **Clarify the non-negotiables upfront.** Be clear about the specific data or format you need, so there's no confusion about the essentials.

- **Give space for creativity where it makes sense.** Let them decide how to structure or present the information in a way that feels natural to them.

- **Check in along the way.** Set up a quick midway touchpoint to review progress and make sure the task is on track – this keeps you aligned without micromanaging.

Not much has changed on the surface – you're still asking for the same report. But by connecting it to their motivations and giving them room to contribute in their own way, you're creating an important sense of ownership and purpose. You're showing trust, highlighting their strengths and helping them see how their work matters, all while ensuring you get what you need.

Now, let's say you want to move on from inspiring the team on an individual level and focus on doing it in more public settings, like in team meetings or even presentations. Once you've mastered delegation with purpose in individual tasks, start connecting conversations in wider settings to the company vision. Start presentations by tying your delivery to the company vision first. Centre your communication around connecting actions to a higher purpose, and you'll be well on your way to becoming an inspiring manager.

This shift is important because while individual conversations build trust and connection on a personal level, public settings are where you create a sense of unity and shared purpose.

When you inspire the team collectively, you're not just motivating one person, you're setting the tone for the entire group. It's about showing them how their individual efforts contribute to a bigger picture and encouraging them to see themselves as part of something larger than just their day-to-day tasks.

In these settings, you have the opportunity to:

- **Reinforce the company's vision and mission.** Use team meetings or presentations to remind everyone what you're collectively working towards and why it matters. This helps keep the team aligned and focused on long-term goals.

- **Celebrate shared successes.** Publicly recognising the team's achievements highlights their impact and reinforces the value of their contributions. For example, you might say, 'Our recent launch reached 50,000 users in the first week – that's a huge step towards making technology more accessible for everyone.'

- **Share the 'why' behind decisions.** Explaining the purpose behind initiatives or changes helps the team understand how their work fits into the broader strategy. For instance, 'This new project isn't just about improving user engagement, it's about making our tools even more intuitive, so more people can benefit from what we've built.'

- **Create moments for collaboration.** Public settings allow you to engage the team in discussions about challenges and opportunities. You might say, 'We're facing an exciting challenge here. How do we make this product even more user-friendly? I'd love to hear your ideas on how we can push this forward together.'

By inspiring the team in public settings, you'll be creating a more motivated team that works in a culture of transparency and shared ownership. We want to make sure every team member feels seen, valued and connected to the bigger picture. Not just in their individual roles, but as part of the collective effort.

When done well, these moments ignite a shared energy, showing the team the incredible impact they can achieve when they work together.

> ## 'BUT IT TAKES TOO LONG; I DON'T HAVE THE TIME'
>
> I get it. These more detailed responses, the pauses to include the 'why' before delegating – they're just another thing to add to our busy manager plate, right? It might take three times as many words as the simple ones. But here's the reality: you can either invest a few extra minutes upfront, connecting tasks to a larger purpose, vision and intrinsic motivation, or you can risk much bigger problems down the road, such as:
>
> - an uninspired and disengaged team
> - high staff turnover due to a misalignment of values
> - you feeling frustrated because you're not the inspiring manager you aspire to be
>
> The first option requires just a bit more effort initially, but the second option could cost you far more in the long run.

Create Opportunities for Others

The most inspiring managers don't chase the spotlight; they create it for others. Research on social comparison theory reveals that our brains are naturally wired to compare ourselves to others. This comparison instinct triggers feelings of competition in the workplace, making us see others as rivals rather than allies. For managers, this is a critical insight because, left unchecked, it can lead to behaviours that unintentionally hold people back – like not delegating key opportunities, withholding credit or micromanaging.

But the most effective managers become aware of this as soon as possible and flip the script. Instead of viewing success as a limited resource, they embrace the mindset that there's plenty to go around. They recognise that by helping others succeed, they elevate the entire team, and themselves in the process. When managers focus on lifting others up and creating opportunities for their team to grow and shine, it not only builds trust and loyalty, but also fuels motivation and engagement across the board.

Being aware of this psychological tendency to compete, and choosing to rise above it, is what sets apart truly inspiring leaders. They focus on collaboration over competition, turning their teams into environments where everyone gets opportunities to shine.

I once had the privilege of working under a manager who truly embodied this mindset. Despite us being similar in age, both female and both striving for similar career paths – something that could have easily turned into competition – she went out of her way to support me. She put me forward for speaking events, ensured my salary was always where it needed to be and spoke positively about me in rooms I wasn't in.

Not only did I see her as really inspiring me and making me feel valued, but it motivated me to work harder and step up in ways I might not have otherwise. Her belief in me gave me the confidence to tackle challenges head-on, because I knew I always had her unwavering support.

When you link your team's work to intrinsic motivations and give people opportunities to excel, you naturally inspire them to go the extra mile. This highlights how powerful it can be to not only delegate, but also actively create opportunities for your team to grow alongside that.

So, how can you start creating these moments?

- **Be generous with credit.** When someone contributes meaningfully, make sure their efforts are recognised publicly.

- **Push them outside their comfort zone.** Encourage team members to take on projects or opportunities that stretch their skills and confidence, but make sure they know you've got their back.

- **Look for untapped potential.** Look for team members who haven't had a chance to showcase their skills or take on bigger responsibilities yet. Consider who could benefit from stepping into the spotlight and think about specific opportunities – like leading a project, presenting in a meeting or taking ownership of a new initiative – that could help them grow and build their confidence.

- **Take time to celebrate success.** It's easy to assume praise is a given, but in the rush of daily tasks, it's something we often overlook. Make it a priority to recognise your team's great work – it goes further than you think in building morale and motivation.

When you create opportunities for others to shine, your team flourishes, and so do you. The best leaders inspire not by hogging the limelight, but by using it to showcase the incredible talent around them.

The journey to becoming an inspiring leader may seem daunting, especially when compared to icons like Oprah Winfrey or Nelson Mandela. But, hopefully, through this

Growth isn't a competition; there is room for everyone to win.

chapter, you have learned that inspiration isn't reserved for a select few – it's a skill you can learn and master. By connecting your team's work to their values and a shared mission, delegating with purpose and creating opportunities for others, you'll not only inspire your team, but also leave a lasting impact on your organisation and skyrocket your own career.

While what we've explored in this chapter is a real cheat code in becoming the manager people see as 'inspiring', truly being an inspiring manager is about much more than just giving purpose-connected tasks. It's about really embodying qualities that resonate deeply with your team; qualities that make them want to follow you not just because they have to, but because they genuinely want to. It's about creating an atmosphere where your team feels valued, trusted and empowered to contribute their best work.

But inspiration alone isn't enough – you also need to steer the ship in the right direction. The best managers don't just lead people, they lead with vision. And that starts with thinking strategically.

Embrace the Big Picture: Thinking Strategically

When I was working in my first proper management role on the Harrods shop floor, I would come into work each day in 'firefighting' mode. I'd step onto the shop floor and immediately allow myself to be pulled in multiple different directions with new requests, updates and last-minute changes that seemed to come out of nowhere. Each new problem caused my anxiety to spike. I'd jump in and tackle each issue as it came with the same speed and urgency as the last, and it felt like I was doing my best just to stay afloat.

One busy morning stands out. My team was under pressure to meet a sales target by the end of the week, and I spent hours frantically rearranging staff schedules to ensure we had our strongest performers on the highest-value shifts. I repositioned team members to cover areas where we were seeing the most customer traffic and asked others to focus on upselling to maximise every interaction. All the while, I nervously monitored exchanges with customers, stepping in to coach staff mid-task and checking in on everyone regularly to make sure we were hitting the numbers. By the end of the day, we were inching closer to our target, but I felt absolutely drained. And, despite the effort, I knew that, even if we did get there, come next week, we'd just be in the same chaotic situation.

Looking back, I can see how much I was caught up in the urgency of the moment rather than having a clear sense of direction. I was fuelled by anxiety and this nagging fear of failure. I felt like every problem was a test of my ability to lead, and the thought of letting down the team or missing the target completely overwhelmed me. Even when something wasn't actually urgent, it felt urgent because I was so caught up in the pressure of the day. I'd drop everything to tackle whatever was going wrong, convinced I had to sort it myself, only to find another fire waiting for me straight after. I hadn't yet figured out how to step back, take a breath and look at things in a more strategic, long-term way.

Strategic thinking is the ability to see beyond the immediate tasks and focus on the bigger picture: aligning the day-to-day actions of the team with the organisation's long-term goals and mission. Leaders who think strategically aren't just managing incoming situations, they steer, ensuring that their teams' efforts are consistently pushing towards the overarching goals. Successful leaders understand that strategic thinking involves assessing the current situation, anticipating future opportunities and challenges, and developing effective strategies to navigate these.

Back then, if I'd been thinking strategically, instead of scrambling to meet each week's sales goal, I could have taken a step back to look at the patterns causing the shortfalls and invested time in setting up stronger processes, training or team structures to prevent these issues from repeating. Yes, it might have meant pulling away from some of the firefighting tasks; maybe we'd have missed the target for a couple of weeks at the beginning, and potentially a few of those 'urgent' things might even have been missed. But, rather than simply reacting, I could have focused on creating a foundation for *sustainable* success, which ultimately would have made each busy day on the floor easier to manage for both me and the team.

Rosalind Brewer, former CEO of Walgreens Boots Alliance, is an inspiring example of how strategic thinking can turn crisis into a growth opportunity. Brewer joined Walgreens in 2021, during one of the most challenging periods in recent healthcare history. With the COVID-19 pandemic spreading rapidly, Walgreens faced unprecedented demand as both a pharmacy and a healthcare provider responsible for distributing vaccines and keeping communities safe. Brewer could easily have just seen this as a logistical challenge to be tackled on a day-to-day basis – fighting the fires as they started to rise. But in an interview with Hoda Kotb on the *TODAY Show*, Brewer discussed her approach to business and life, highlighting her vision for Walgreens Boots Alliance during the pandemic.

Instead of focusing solely on the immediate needs of vaccine distribution, Brewer approached the situation with a broader, strategic mindset to make Walgreens a central player in accessible healthcare. During the pandemic, Walgreens became a key distributor of COVID-19 vaccines, launching off-site vaccination clinics in underserved areas and partnering with healthcare providers and government agencies to increase vaccine equity. These efforts helped cement Walgreens' role in accessible healthcare. The company also invested in telehealth services and opened health hubs that provided convenient access to testing, treatment and advice. The infrastructure and partnerships built during this time allowed Walgreens to continue offering an expanded range of vaccination services, which now includes streamlined access to vaccines in stores and through community-based clinics. This expansion has had a lasting impact on how Walgreens delivers health services today.

By broadening Walgreens' role in healthcare, Brewer not only addressed an urgent need during the pandemic, but also created a foundation for long-term growth and innovation. Brewer didn't just ask, 'How do we get through this crisis?', she asked, 'How can we turn this into an opportunity that *builds* our future?' This mindset shift is the essence of strategic thinking, reminding us that each decision should not only solve today's challenges, but contribute to long-term success.

As managers, we can learn from Brewer's approach by considering how our actions today align with the long-term vision.

Building Your Strategic Thinking Skills

We've seen how becoming a strategic thinker is about consistently choosing the long-term gain over the immediate win. So, here are a few practical actions that helped me shift my mindset and develop the skills to think and act strategically:

PAUSE TO DIAGNOSE THE ROOT CAUSE

In my early days on the Harrods shop floor, I was always ready to jump in and fix whatever problem came my way. But I learned that to think strategically, you need to slow down and ask, *Why is this happening?* Instead of just responding to the surface issue, take a moment to understand what's creating the challenge. For example, if your team is consistently struggling to meet deadlines, ask, *Is it a workload issue? Are priorities unclear? Or is it a training gap?* By diagnosing the root cause, you can address the real problem and stop the pattern from repeating.

EVALUATE THE IMPACT BEFORE ACTING

Strategic thinking requires prioritising what will have the biggest impact. Before you act, consider:

- What's the potential outcome if I do (or don't) address this issue?

- How does this align with our team's broader goals?

- Is this urgent, or does it just feel urgent in the moment?

For example, if a client escalates an issue, it's tempting to drop everything and fix it. But stepping back and evaluating the long-term impact might lead you to involve someone else or make a decision that prevents the same escalation in the future.

FOCUS ON BUILDING SYSTEMS, NOT JUST SOLVING PROBLEMS

Early on, I was constantly firefighting because I wasn't thinking about systems. Strategic thinkers focus on creating repeatable processes to avoid future chaos. If you're always reshuffling schedules to meet targets, ask yourself: *Can we build a scheduling process that anticipates peaks in demand? Do we need a better way to track sales performance in real time?* By implementing systems, you free up your mental bandwidth and create stability for the team (we'll cover everything systems in the second section of this book).

INVOLVE YOUR TEAM IN PROBLEM-SOLVING

Strategic thinking doesn't mean you have to figure out everything on your own. A huge shift for me came when I started involving my team in the process. Instead of micromanaging or taking everything on myself, I'd ask questions like:

- 'What do you think is causing this problem?'

- 'What would you suggest we do differently next time?'

- 'How can we prevent this from happening again?'

This not only lightens your load, but also empowers your team to think strategically themselves, creating a stronger, more proactive group overall.

By learning to ask better questions, evaluate the bigger picture and involve your team, you can start shifting your focus from simply reacting to building long-term solutions. But strategic thinking doesn't happen in a vacuum, it's often tested the most when the vision you're working towards keeps changing.

Navigating Change from Above

Let's be honest, it's one thing to focus on strategic thinking when you're the one setting the direction, but what about when the vision coming from above keeps shifting? For most managers, this is the messy reality. Decisions change, priorities get reshuffled and new initiatives seem to land on our desk out of nowhere. It can feel like you're stuck in firefighting mode, reacting to updates instead of having the space to lead with any kind of strategy.

The truth is, to lead strategically, we do need to figure out how to navigate all this change. Even when the bigger picture feels unpredictable, how you communicate and manage those shifts with your team can make or break your success. Strategic thinking is never about avoiding change, but more about guiding your team through it while staying true to your goals and supporting the organisation's long-term vision. Let's explore how to handle this kind of change effectively, without letting it derail your team's focus.

In the early years of my career, I vividly remember a time when senior management introduced a sudden shift in our sales strategy. Overnight, we were told to focus entirely on upselling a specific product line, with little explanation about why this change was happening or how it aligned with our broader goals. Instead of pausing to understand the reasoning or asking questions, I let my frustration take over. I vented to my team about how unfair it was, unintentionally passing on my negativity, and then threw myself into 'fix-it' mode. I scrambled to adjust schedules, push targets and demand more from everyone without really thinking about how to communicate the change effectively or motivate the team.

Looking back, this was exactly what *not* to do. Firstly, my emotional reaction not only added stress for me, it also created confusion and frustration for the team. And as we learned in Chapter 1, we never want our emotions to own us. Secondly, by focusing on the immediate tasks without helping them see the bigger picture or providing clear guidance, I undermined their trust and left them feeling just as reactive as I was.

To navigate change strategically in your team, consider the following steps:

GET CLARITY FROM YOUR SENIORS

When new directions come from above, take the time to fully understand them before bringing them to your team. Ask questions like, 'Why is this change happening now?' or 'How does this fit into the company's long-term vision?' Engaging with senior leadership ensures you're clear on the 'why' behind the decision, allowing you to frame it for your team in a way that makes sense.

In my early years as a leader, I would rush to share news without fully understanding it myself. I'd get caught up in the drama, sometimes venting to my team with comments like, 'I can't believe they've done this again.' But that only created more stress and uncertainty, as well as undermining the leadership team. Now, I make sure to gather the full context first, even if it means asking questions that feel uncomfortable. Once I'm clear (and less emotional), I can guide my team with confidence and transparency.

PAUSE AND PREPARE

Once you've gained clarity from your seniors, take a moment to pause and think strategically about how to communicate this to your team. Just like with all EI, the pause is essential to avoid reacting emotionally or passing on unnecessary stress. Focus on sharing the key headlines: why this direction is happening, how it aligns with broader goals and what it means for the team.

For example, instead of saying, 'Here we go again with

another change; I can't believe X manager has done this,' reframe it as, 'The company is shifting direction to focus on X, which supports our long-term goals. Here's how this affects us, and here's what we'll do to adapt.'

This level of clarity can only come after taking the time to process the information yourself. It's also okay to acknowledge when something feels difficult or unfair, without being negative. You might say, 'I know this is a big adjustment and adds more to your plate, but I appreciate your effort as we work through it together.' Honest but reassuring communication builds trust and credibility as a leader.

BE THE FILTER

When being strategic in navigating change from above, the team doesn't need to hear every detail or minor update – your role is to filter out the noise and focus on what matters most. Share only what directly impacts their work and frame it in a way that's clear and actionable.

For instance, instead of sending out updates as soon as you hear something, wait until you have a full understanding of what's happening and how it will affect your team. Then present the information calmly, focusing on what they need to know and how they should act. This ensures your team stays aligned, informed and focused, without feeling overwhelmed by unnecessary details.

STAY CALM

When things feel uncertain, your team needs more than just clear direction – they need a manager who can stay calm and composed, even when things get tricky. If you let stress or frustration show through too much in times like these, it can ripple through the team, making everything feel much more overwhelming.

But let's be real. Staying calm isn't easy. We're human, and the pressure to keep it together can sometimes feel like a lot. You're not a robot, and you'll have moments when it's tough to stay composed. That's okay. What matters is how you handle those moments and how you reset.

Before talking to your team about a tough situation, take a minute to gather yourself. You don't need to pretend everything's fine if it isn't, but how you frame things makes all the difference. For example, in the past I've said things like, 'I know this is a big ask, and I'm feeling it too, but here's how we're going to work through it together.' That mix of honesty and reassurance builds trust and keeps everyone focused.

It's never about being perfect. It's about being steady and showing your team they can count on you, even when things are challenging. Staying calm sets the tone and creates the kind of environment where people can think clearly, work effectively and feel supported – even when the pressure is on.

Give Yourself Healthy Limits

I often felt as though I needed to be available, adaptable and ready to take on anything to fix problems and support my team, but in order to think strategically and focus on that bigger picture, we have to actually make space for it. Being strategic is as much about ruthlessly saying no when you know unimportant tasks are getting in the way as it is about thinking long term. We have to set limits to protect time for strategic planning. We have to push back. Without boundaries, we spread ourselves too thin and get caught up in endless decision-making, chasing every opportunity without focus.

Setting intentional limits on our time, resources and energy allows us to prioritise what truly matters, including staying focused on those long-term goals, and preventing burnout along the way. Strategic leaders understand that saying yes to everything dilutes focus and can hinder progress. Instead, they learn to set boundaries that guide their efforts in an intentional direction.

Successful leaders understand that limits create focus. In a world of limitless options, constraints force prioritisation and clarity. By setting boundaries around their time, resources or choices, they allow themselves and their teams to concentrate on what will drive long-term success. Instead of getting pulled in every direction by short-term opportunities, limits provide a framework for focusing on what has the greatest strategic impact, keeping the team aligned with long-term goals.

This concept of constraint-based productivity is supported by research, such as the 'paradox of choice', a term coined by psychologist Barry Schwartz. Schwartz found that an excess of options can lead to decision paralysis and dissatisfaction. For leaders, the more choices and responsibilities we take on, the more likely we are to experience these effects, making us less effective and clouding our long-term vision. Setting limits reduces this cognitive load, keeping leaders clear-headed and focused on the most strategic goals.

We can also see this in real-world examples. Steve Jobs famously restricted Apple's product line to a few key offerings, focusing on quality and innovation rather than expanding into endless categories. Jobs understood that by limiting options, he was forcing the team to excel within those boundaries, which ultimately led to some of Apple's most iconic products. This constraint-driven approach is credited with Apple's long-term success, as it allowed the team to direct their energy towards a few carefully chosen priorities rather than spreading it thinly across numerous projects.

Psychologist Adam Grant, in his book *Originals: How nonconformists move the world*, discusses how constraints can actually enhance creativity. He explains that limitations force individuals and teams to think differently, leading to more innovative solutions. By setting clear boundaries, leaders can create an environment where their teams are encouraged to innovate within set parameters, effectively working towards long-term goals even with limited resources.

> *Successful leaders recognise that constraints can sharpen focus by simplifying decision-making, clarifying priorities and driving both quality and creativity.*

When you're not trying to be everywhere and do everything, you can concentrate your efforts where they matter most, making a significant impact on what truly counts in the long run.

Let's discuss practical ways you can incorporate limits into the management of your team:

DEADLINES AREN'T RESTRICTIONS

When I was managing my team at Harrods, I thought giving them complete flexibility with deadlines would create a more relaxed and empowered environment. I assumed that without time constraints, they'd feel more freedom and autonomy. But it didn't quite work out that way. Without clear timelines, progress often slowed, and it became hard for everyone to prioritise their tasks. We'd end up scrambling at the last minute to meet targets, creating unnecessary stress and chaos.

Over time, I realised that deadlines don't just keep track of time, they help us create focus. Once I began setting clear timelines, things started to change. Deadlines gave us the framework we needed to stay on track and actually get things done.

Research supports this too. A study in the *Journal of Applied Psychology* found that teams' shared temporal cognition – that is, team members' shared understanding of timelines and deadlines – positively influences team performance, coordination, and meeting deadlines.

The key, though, is to set deadlines collaboratively – instead of simply handing them down, bring the team into the process. Ask for their input, agree on what's realistic and get their commitment to the deadlines.

Deadlines, when approached in the right way, shouldn't feel like pressure or control. They're a tool to create clarity, structure and a sense of shared purpose that keeps everyone moving in the right direction.

BE SELECTIVE WITH RESOURCES

At GoProposal, we were a lean operation with no external investment – meaning that every penny had to be spent wisely. This constraint initially felt like a challenge, but it turned out to be a blessing in disguise. With limited resources, we had no option but to focus on what mattered most. For example, instead of throwing large, costly events to attract new clients, we redirected our efforts towards hosting smaller, intimate gatherings with our existing customers. The results were remarkable. By investing in our current clients, we built loyalty and community – a far more sustainable strategy than constantly chasing new leads.

Having large amounts of resources can actually be a curse if it leads to wasteful spending or scattered focus. When resources are abundant, it's easy to fall into the trap of taking on too many projects, trying every new idea or overspending without a clear strategy. With too much money or time, we're tempted to 'do it all', but this often dilutes our efforts and reduces impact. A surplus can lead to a lack of urgency, pushing teams to make impulsive choices simply because the means are available.

Working within resource limits forces us to be strategic, creative and intentional with every decision. When we know resources are limited, we need to prioritise the actions that will bring the highest return. Instead of simply 'doing more', we do *what matters*. When forced to make the most out of less, teams learn to find smarter ways to reach their goals. It encourages them to develop sustainable approaches, concentrate on what builds long-term value and creatively solve problems.

REDUCE CHOICES FOR BETTER DECISIONS

Instead of trying to weigh up endless options, focus on narrowing down choices to three viable ones. This approach leads to better outcomes strategically because it reduces the overwhelm that comes with too many possibilities. Saying yes to fewer things creates space to fully commit to what truly matters, helping you and your team stay focused on the long-term horizon.

Here are some strategies for narrowing down options quickly:

- **Limit the option-gathering phase.** Set a clear time limit for brainstorming or gathering potential solutions. For example, you might say, 'Let's take 15 minutes to identify possible ideas, then we'll filter them down.' This prevents the process from dragging on and keeps discussions focused.

- **Use prioritisation criteria.** Establish clear criteria for what makes an option viable. Ask questions like, 'Does this align with our goals? Does it fit within our budget or resources? Can we realistically execute it within the given timeframe?' Filtering options through these questions helps you rule out anything that doesn't meet the key requirements.

- **Seek input from your team.** Bring your team into the process by asking them to vote on or rank their top three choices based on impact and feasibility. Collaborative input not only speeds up the narrowing down process, but also ensures buy-in for the final decision.

By reducing choices, we aren't cutting corners; we are focusing our energy on what really matters. By limiting options to the best three and following a clear, collaborative process, we will not only save time, but also make decisions that are more intentional and impactful in the long run.

Embracing Your New Strategic Mindset

In its simplest form, strategic thinking is about shifting your perspective from daily tasks to long-term goals. As a manager, this means focusing on how your actions contribute to the mission of your team, your company and even your future self, even when challenges arise. If I'd approached my early days at Harrods with a strategic mindset, I would have focused less on firefighting and more on setting up the structures to prevent those issues in the first place.

Building a strategic mindset involves fighting to be curious under pressure, balancing freedom with limits for your team and navigating change with confidence. By making this shift, you'll enhance your team's performance and position yourself as a leader who drives sustained success.

Strategic thinking is all about making focused, purposeful choices, from setting limits to navigating change. But even with the clearest vision and the best-planned strategies, not every decision will go perfectly. In fact, the most impactful growth often happens through our setbacks. As we refine our strategies and set thoughtful limits, we must also learn to embrace failure as part of the process. In the next chapter, we'll explore why embracing failure is essential for leadership, how it builds resilience and creates safety, and how we can create a culture where mistakes aren't just accepted but powerfully encouraged.

Don't Play the Superhero: Embrace Failure

As managers, we are so often *terrified* of failure because of the immense pressure we're under to deliver results, meet expectations and maintain our team's reputation. There's a belief that mistakes will reflect poorly on us as leaders, signalling incompetence or a lack of control. This fear is then heightened by the company cultures that punish failure (rather than see it as part of the learning process).

Additionally, many managers worry that allowing failure will damage team morale, delay progress or risk their standing with upper management. And, as a result, they focus on avoiding mistakes instead of embracing failure as an opportunity for growth, innovation and development. So instead of embracing failure, we become what's known as a 'rescuer'.

The idea of a *rescuer* comes from Transactional Analysis, specifically the Drama Triangle, a 1960s concept by Dr Stephen Karpman. In this model, a rescuer is someone who steps in to 'save' others, solving problems for people in their life and protecting them from mistakes, instead of letting them handle challenges themselves.

A rescuer in management is someone who steps in to solve problems for their team, shielding them from failure. While the intention is to help, 'rescuing' instead prevents team members from learning, growing and taking ownership of their work, ultimately hindering their development.

It took me way too long into my management career to realise I was being a 'rescuer'. When I was in the marketing manager role at GoProposal, I had just hired a social media manager into my team – let's call her Sarah – an ambitious and talented team member. Within a year, I moved up into director of operations and she was promoted into the marketing manager role.

Naturally, I wanted her to succeed, especially in front of the founder. This happens a lot when we hire someone – we have bias towards making it work out for them. So I started stepping in, tweaking her work before it went out and guiding her during meetings on what to say to look good. My intentions were in the right place, but, in my eagerness to shield her from failure, I inadvertently stunted her growth.

It dawned on me one day, after a particularly intense meeting, when once again I had stepped in and spoken for her, that I wasn't allowing Sarah to learn. Instead of giving her the space to try, fail and grow, I was ensuring she looked polished and never had to deal with any of the difficult stuff, but it was at the expense of her learning journey.

This approach, I realised, wasn't sustainable for either of us. By not letting her find her own way, I wasn't creating resilience or psychological safety: two critical components of high-performing teams.

Many of us fall into the trap of rescuing our team. But rescuing is a short-term fix that will do you a long-term disservice.

Redefining Failure

'Failure' is a loaded word, but there are upsides to falling short of our goals sometimes. Let me share a lesson from a personal experience.

Keeping physically fit is a huge priority of mine, but at the same time every year, when the colder, darker mornings set in, I find it harder to maintain the discipline to get to the gym. So, last November, I hired a personal trainer to help keep me accountable during those tricky months.

The biggest lesson I learned from my trainer wasn't a physical one; it was a mindset shift. Within the walls of the gym, 'failure' has an entirely different meaning. When you push yourself through an exercise to the point of failure – where your muscles physically can't lift, push or pull any further – you're effectively causing tiny tears in the muscle fibres. And while that might sound negative, it's actually the foundation of how muscles grow stronger. These small tears trigger your body's natural repair process. As the fibres rebuild, they grow back thicker and more resilient, making the muscle stronger than it was before.

This kind of failure is celebrated and encouraged. You push yourself to the point of failure because that's where the most growth happens in your muscles. In fact, every session, your goal is to fail because only then do you know you've pushed as hard as you can.

The word 'fail' is thrown around so often in the gym that it now has a completely different meaning in my head. I began to see failure as a target rather than a defeat. And the more I thought about it, the more I realised how powerful this mindset could be in leadership.

83

FAILURE IN LEADERSHIP

The best businesses aim to 'out-fail' their competitors. Sounds counterintuitive, right? But think about it. The companies that innovate, take risks and aren't afraid of getting it wrong are the ones that push boundaries and ultimately succeed. They're not playing it safe; they're out there failing faster and learning more than their risk-averse counterparts.

One of the best real-world examples of a company that embraces failure as part of its strategy is Amazon. Under Jeff Bezos' leadership, Amazon has consistently encouraged risk-taking and experimentation, even if it leads to failure. Bezos famously said, 'If you're going to take bold bets, they're going to be experiments. And if they're experiments, you don't know ahead of time if they're going to work.'

When Amazon launched the Fire Phone in 2014, they were hoping to make a big splash in the smartphone market. But, let's face it, it was a flop. The phone didn't take off due to a mix of high pricing, lack of standout features and poor integration with existing platforms like Android and iOS. Within a year, it was discontinued, and Amazon had to write off millions.

Now, here's where it gets interesting. Instead of letting this failure discourage the team or push them into the shadows, Jeff Bezos handled it differently. He told Ian Freed, the executive in charge of the Fire Phone, 'You can't, for one minute, feel bad about the Fire Phone. Promise me you won't lose a minute of sleep.' That approach set the tone for how failure was viewed at Amazon – not as something to hide from, but as a chance to learn and pivot.

Bezos' attitude shows how powerful it is to embrace failure and support your team through it. By treating it as a learning opportunity, Amazon kept their people motivated, avoided a blame game and used the experience to fuel innovation. Failure wasn't just tolerated at Amazon; it was actively reframed as part of the process, which is why they were able to turn a misstep into a breakthrough.

The Fire Phone featured advanced technologies like 3D head-tracking and voice recognition. While these features weren't enough to save the phone, the voice technology, in particular, was a key learning point. Amazon took this voice-control expertise and redirected it into developing Alexa.

One of the biggest takeaways from the Fire Phone's failure was the importance of understanding customer needs. Bezos realised they had pushed a product that didn't solve a core customer problem because they already had more affordable solutions. This failure pushed them to focus more on how they could add real value to customers' lives, leading to the creation of Amazon Echo, a voice-activated smart speaker that was built around convenience and a new kind of accessible home automation.

By allowing room for bold risks and failure, Amazon, under Bezos' leadership, has been able to stay ahead of competitors, innovate and remain a market leader. Their willingness to fail fast, learn and adapt is a core part of their strategy that has driven long-term success.

Let's go back to Sarah. By not letting her fail, I was holding her back and limiting what our team could achieve. If I'd stepped back and let her handle that meeting on her own, even if it got awkward for a moment, it could have been a chance for her to shine. Maybe she'd have said, 'I don't have the full answer right now, but here's what I think we could try' or asked a question to the group that sparked a better discussion. That moment of figuring things out for herself could've given her more confidence and even led us to a new idea we hadn't thought of.

When we embrace failure, both individually and as a team, we create an environment where people feel safe to try, mess up and learn from it. That's when the real magic happens – when your team feels comfortable enough to take risks, bring fresh ideas to the table and grow in ways you wouldn't expect.

There's research to back this up too. A study published in the *Harvard Business Review* analysed organisations across various industries and found that those with a high tolerance for failure experienced 30 per cent higher revenue growth on average compared to their more cautious competitors. These companies create cultures of psychological safety, where employees feel empowered to innovate and solve problems without the fear of punishment. The study emphasised that this mindset not only improves short-term creativity, but also drives long-term strategic gains.

How to Practically Encourage Failure in Your Team

Talking about embracing failure is easy, but putting it into action is where the real challenge lies.

Even after I realised I was rescuing Sarah, it was a long road to undo those ingrained behaviours. I wanted to help her succeed so badly that I kept stepping in to prevent any slip-ups, even though I knew it was holding her back. Recognising you're a rescuer is the first step, but changing those habits takes time and intentional effort. As I learned, just knowing that failure is essential isn't enough – you need to commit to embedding it into your team's day-to-day work. You need practical steps that encourage failure in a way that drives growth, not fear.

So, as always with this book, let's go into some of the practical ways I found success with embracing failure, and how they can work for you too. You can start doing these today and, over time, they'll help undo some of those rescuer tendencies. The key is to make failure a natural, accepted part of your strategy, even when it feels tough, and the wins will soon follow.

Here are three ways you can get started this week:

1. BUILD FAILURE INTO REPORTING

When we're reporting on targets, wins, losses, and so on, rather than focusing solely on the normal business KPIs, integrate failure in there too. A simple way to do this is by structuring your team's monthly check-ins around three main questions:

1. What went well, and how can we do more of it?

2. What didn't go well, and what can we learn from it?

3. What are we experimenting with this month?

These questions create a balanced conversation where failures are as important as wins. We're actually pre-empting and rewarding experimentation, no matter the result.

By discussing what didn't go as planned, you're sending a clear message that failure is a learning opportunity, not something to be brushed under the rug. This builds a culture of openness and encourages team members to take risks without the fear of blame.

You'll find that accountability and transparency are key when it comes to normalising failure, and the soft skills in Rules #2 and #6 can be really helpful for making this reporting structure successful for your team. We'll also go deeper into building hard skills and practical strategies for keeping ourselves and our team accountable in Rule #15.

2. START A REJECTION LOG

If you're not hearing 'no' very often, you're not aiming high enough. I still to this day keep a rejection log. The idea is simple: track every rejection you or your team receives, and make sure that you are regularly receiving them. It might sound counterintuitive, but if you're always hearing 'yes', you're playing it too safe.

For me today, rejection often looks like approaching major brands for partnerships, selling products into corporates or posting videos on social media with little reaction. Nine times out of ten, I am met with rejection. But that one 'yes' makes all the difference, opening doors to opportunities we never thought possible. That one yes propels you so far forward. But we have to push and push for the 'no's too. Part of that push is learning to handle ambiguous responses like 'Maybe' or 'We'll think about it.' These grey areas can leave us stuck and hesitant, but persistence is key. Following up with clarity and purpose – whether through emails, calls or meetings – can help move the conversation forward to a definitive answer, whether it's a yes or a no. That resolution is what allows you to focus your energy on the next opportunity.

Encourage your team to log and celebrate their rejections, knowing that every 'no' brings them closer to the right 'yes'.

Over time, this shifts their mindset to see rejection – and failure – as part of the journey towards success.

3. IGNORE YOUR COMPETITION

As leaders in business, we're subconsciously taught to feel pressure to compete, not just as businesses against outside companies, but within our own organisations too. It's easy to fall into the trap of comparing your team's performance to other departments, measuring your progress against colleagues going for similar roles or constantly looking over your shoulder at industry rivals. This competitive mindset can push us towards playing it safe, focusing on quick wins to keep up rather than making the bold decisions that lead to long-term success.

I struggled with this early in my leadership journey. In the role of marketing manager, it became so easy to constantly spy on what my competitors were doing; checking in to see how their latest campaign had performed compared to ours, what new social media trends they were hopping on, and so on.

I used to feel this constant sense of envy and frustration watching what our competitors were up to. It felt like we were always chasing them, trying to keep up. Then, one day, I just decided enough was enough – I blocked them on social media. Out of sight out of mind, right? As soon as I stopped focusing on what they were doing and turned my attention to my own team's unique vision, everything shifted. We suddenly had the space to take risks, make mistakes and learn without the pressure of feeling like we were falling behind. That's when the real innovation started.

This idea ties into the concept of the 'infinite game', first introduced by philosopher James P. Carse in his 1986 book *Finite and Infinite Games*. Carse distinguishes between finite games, which have set rules, clear winners and losers, and a defined endpoint, and infinite games, where the goal is not to win but to keep playing, evolving and growing. In leadership, playing an infinite game means focusing on long-term progress and continuous improvement, rather than just trying to beat others in the short term.

By playing the infinite game, I shifted my mindset from competing against others to striving for constant growth. It wasn't about being the best today; it was about building a team and business that would keep adapting and growing well into the future. When you stop comparing yourself to others, you create a space where failure is not something to be feared, because we're not always trying to keep up with another company or person – ultimately allowing your team to take risks, innovate and lead without the constraints of competition holding them back.

Author and leadership expert Simon Sinek later expanded on this idea in his book *The Infinite Game*, explaining that leaders who adopt this mindset are better equipped to thrive in the long term, focusing on innovation and sustainable success rather than simply trying to outdo their competition. This shift can create more resilient, forward-thinking teams that aren't afraid to embrace failure as a future stepping stone to greatness.

Create Psychological Safety for Your Team

Psychological safety is the ultimate goal in leadership when it comes to embracing failure. It's the key that unlocks the full potential of a team, allowing them to take risks, make mistakes and innovate without fear. When psychological safety is present, we create an environment where failure becomes a natural and valuable part of the growth process.

The term psychological safety, introduced by Harvard Professor Amy Edmondson, refers to an environment where individuals feel comfortable taking risks, voicing ideas and making mistakes without fear of embarrassment or punishment. In a psychologically safe workplace, people know that failures won't lead to blame or shame, but, instead, provide valuable lessons for improvement. This allows them to work harder and push themselves beyond the edge of their comfort zone.

If your team feels like they'll be criticised for mistakes, they'll avoid risks and innovation. They'll stick to safe, predictable tasks to avoid potential failures.

When you, as a leader, cultivate psychological safety, failure becomes part of the growth process, encouraging your team to take calculated risks and innovate without fear of negative consequences.

Google's Project Aristotle, a comprehensive study of team dynamics, found that psychological safety was *the most critical factor* in a team's success. Teams that felt safe to take risks without fear of retribution were more innovative, collaborative and, ultimately, more successful. Those that lacked this safety often avoided risks, stifling both their creativity and overall performance.

I learned this lesson first-hand when I promoted Sarah all those years ago. I thought I was helping by correcting her work and stepping in when things weren't going well. But what I didn't realise was the message I was sending: that mistakes weren't acceptable and she had to be perfect. It made her cautious, hesitant to take initiative or try anything new.

It wasn't until I stepped back and let her fail that things started to change. Within months, she was handling situations I used to step in for – making decisions on her own and solving problems without needing me to weigh in. By the end of the year, I didn't feel the need to jump in when she paused to answer a tough question. I could see her handling challenges with confidence and, honestly, it was a relief for both of us. Watching her grow like that completely changed how I thought about leadership.

When you build psychological safety into your team's culture, you're protecting them from the fear of failure, giving them the space to experiment, get creative and really thrive.

Your Next Move

As leaders, it's easy to fall into the trap of rescuing our team, just as I did with Sarah. We want them to succeed, so we step in to shield them from failure. But, by doing so, we rob them of the opportunity to grow, learn and become more resilient.

So, next time you find yourself tempted to step in and rescue someone, pause. Let them stumble. Let them fail, and then help them get back up to try again. This doesn't mean leaving them to figure it all out on their own. It's about stepping in as a coach, not a fixer. Start by helping them to reflect on what happened. Ask questions like, 'What do you think went wrong?', 'What would you do differently next time?' or

'What did you learn from this?' to guide them towards their own insights.

From there, work with them to come up with a plan for moving forward. Break down the steps they need to take and ensure they feel supported as they put the plan into action. Be their safety net while allowing them to stay in the driver's seat.

Lastly, acknowledge their efforts and progress, even if the result wasn't perfect. By focusing on the learning and improvement, you'll build their confidence and resilience. When they're able to recover, learn and try again, stronger than before, you'll see the kind of growth that benefits not just them, but the team as a whole.

Finally, it's time for a bit of important reflection. I'd like you to ask yourself the following questions:

1. **How do I react when my team members make mistakes, and what message does that send about failure in our team culture?** Reflect on how your immediate response to failure influences your team's willingness to take risks and innovate.

2. **What steps am I taking to create an environment where my team feels safe to take risks, share ideas and admit failures?** Think about how you're fostering psychological safety. Are there systems in place that encourage open discussions about mistakes and learning from them?

3. **Am I actively stepping back to allow my team to fail and grow, or am I still stepping in as a rescuer?** Reflect on whether you're giving your team the space to

learn from their experiences or if you're inadvertently preventing their growth by always stepping in to fix things.

But creating growth isn't just about creating a safe space to fail. It's also about having the courage to stand firm in your decisions, even when it's uncomfortable. Because at some point, leadership requires making choices that won't make everyone happy.

Rule #6

Choose Respect Over Approval

I spent the first 25 years of my life being a rampant people-pleaser. And I know I'm not the only one. Many of us have felt the need to do things we don't want to do, sacrificing our own sanity for fear of letting others down or being disliked. This desire for approval was ingrained in me, so much so that I wasn't even aware of it most of the time. It was my default mode of operation: say yes to everything, seek validation, avoid conflict.

I felt this constant undercurrent of pressure and a need to pre-empt what others wanted before they even asked. My decisions weren't rooted in what I genuinely thought was best for me, the team or the business; they were driven by what I thought would make other people happy. This often showed up as overcommitting to tasks, staying late to redo work for someone else's approval or smiling and agreeing, even when my gut was screaming no. It would push me to say yes to taking on a new task, even when I knew I had a full workload, because it was unthinkable to say no and potentially have people think I wasn't 'easy to work with' or 'always happy to help'.

But here's the uncomfortable truth: every 'yes' you give to others is you saying a clear 'no' to something else and,

95

often, that something else is far more hidden. As a leader, your attention will be pulled in all different directions and it's more important than ever before to protect your time.

People-pleasers tend to avoid saying no, even when it's clear they're overwhelmed. They jump at every opportunity to help, often at their own expense. They'll downplay their own needs, brush off compliments with self-deprecating remarks or apologise when they've done nothing wrong. Their need to keep the peace often means they won't speak up in meetings, and they might be hesitant to set boundaries, fearing it could rock the boat. The signs are subtle, but once you start noticing the patterns, they're hard to un-see.

Let's imagine an example: Julie is a client account director managing a team and multiple high-value accounts. She agrees to take on additional work for one of her accounts. The task is to lead the marketing launch for a new tech product they've just finished building. On paper, it sounds exciting – an opportunity to impress the boss, get ahead and continue delivering value for this account. The project involves developing a full-scale campaign, managing social media outreach, coordinating with the design team for creative assets and setting up a launch event. Julie can already imagine the kudos she'll get if the campaign is a success. Saying no feels like she would be letting them down or missing a chance to prove herself.

But, in reality, she is already overseeing two other major projects for this account. And, deep down, she knows she's stretching herself too thin. She can see the warning signs: her calendar is booked solid with back-to-back meetings, she has to catch up on emails at 9pm and her to-do list seems never-ending.

She thought saying yes would show dedication and commitment, but, instead, it's leading to her feeling like walking death, being frustrated, resenting work and delivering subpar results in every other area she is trying to manage. She isn't impressing anyone. All she is showing is that she doesn't know how to set boundaries.

That's how the people-pleaser's trap works: you say yes to avoid disappointment in the short term, but the long-term effects are far worse.

And the irony? All that approval you are chasing never feels satisfying. It is temporary, fleeting and, ultimately, unfulfilling.

The impact of people-pleasing doesn't stop at just you. In this example, as a result, Julie's team is massively affected. Though she tries to protect them from the additional work, the reality is she ends up having to delegate parts of it to them anyway as the workload is unmanageable. It leads to last-minute demands on them, endless revisions and rising frustrations for everyone involved.

Your inability to push back or set boundaries doesn't just stretch you too thin – it drags your team along, causing stress and burnout for all.

Saying yes when we shouldn't can have ripple effects, leaving our direct reports stretched, stressed and unable to do their best work. If we want to avoid falling into the people-pleaser's trap, we have to lead by example and protect our teams just as much as we protect ourselves.

I remember finally understanding the power of 'no' and the importance of letting go of seeking approval. It was during yet another late night in the office. I was sitting at my desk, completely drained, with an unfinished project in front of me and an email from my manager asking me to take on yet another 'urgent' task. I stared at the screen for what felt like an eternity, my stomach twisting into knots. I knew I couldn't do it – not without sacrificing my health or letting something else fall through the cracks.

For the first time, I typed out a response that started with the word 'no'. I explained that my plate was already full and I wouldn't be able to take on the additional project without compromising the quality of my current work. I hesitated before hitting send, replaying worst-case scenarios in my mind: *What if they think I'm lazy? What if this ruins my reputation? What if I'm seen as difficult?*

But when the reply came back, all it said was: 'Thanks for letting me know – let's find someone else to take this on.' That was it. No drama. No backlash. The negative outcomes I'd feared didn't happen. In fact, I felt a huge sense of relief and even a little pride for standing my ground. It was such a simple moment, but it shifted everything for me. I realised how much I'd been overthinking and how often I'd been saying yes out of fear rather than logic.

And here's what's most important: I discovered that saying no didn't mean I became disliked or missed out on important opportunities to get ahead. Quite the opposite, in fact. By being clear about my limits and focusing on doing fewer things exceptionally well, I started to deliver stronger results. My work became more impactful, and the quality of my contributions stood out in ways it hadn't when I was spreading myself too thin.

And the change didn't stop with me. As I began setting clear boundaries, my team noticed a significant shift in our work dynamics. They experienced fewer last-minute pressures and were encouraged to prioritise tasks more effectively, leading to a noticeable boost in both morale and productivity. In learning to say no, I not only reclaimed my own focus and well-being, but also created an environment where my team felt empowered to manage their workload and collaborate more efficiently. Ultimately, by protecting our time and energy, we all benefited, proving that healthy boundaries can drive success for everyone involved.

Instead of being seen as a weakness, my ability to say no became a strength. It showed my peers and superiors that I had the confidence to prioritise and the foresight to protect my capacity. While it may have meant passing on some opportunities, the trade-off was worth it. The opportunities I did take on were the ones that aligned with my strengths (something we'll be exploring in depth in Rule #9) and allowed me to truly excel. And the respect I gained – from my superiors, my team and, crucially, myself – far outweighed any fear I had of missing out.

Shifting Focus: From Pleasing to Leading

It's natural, especially when you're new to a management role, to want to be liked by your team. After all, a harmonious, friendly environment feels good. You might think that if your team likes you, they'll work harder, be more cooperative and contribute more. But that's only half the picture.

Here's the harsh reality: you can't be everyone's friend and an effective leader at the same time.

Yes, you can be approachable, compassionate and supportive, but there will be times when you have to make tough decisions. There will be times when people will dislike those decisions, and that's okay. As a manager, your job isn't to win a popularity contest; it's to lead with integrity and purpose.

RESPECT > APPROVAL

Respect has a tangible impact – not only on your team relationships, but also on the broader success of your organisation. Earning respect from your team drives their commitment, engagement and loyalty.

As a result, it's crucial to shift our focus from winning short-term approval or being 'liked' to building long-term respect. Chasing approval can feel rewarding in the moment – a nod of agreement in a meeting, praise from your boss or a quick show of gratitude from your team. But approval is fleeting, often tied to temporary emotions or superficial gestures. It doesn't create the foundation of trust or credibility that true leadership demands.

Building respect, on the other hand, requires patience, consistency and often the courage to make decisions that might not be popular in the short term. It's about holding your team accountable, setting clear boundaries and showing up authentically, even when that means having difficult conversations or making choices that won't immediately please everyone. Respect isn't earned by avoiding conflict or saying yes to everything. It's earned by staying true to your values and leading with integrity.

When you focus on respect, you're investing in something far more enduring than approval. You're creating a culture where your team trusts your judgement, believes in your fairness and feels confident in your leadership. Over time, this leads to stronger relationships, higher performance and a more engaged, committed team.

So, the next time you find yourself tempted to prioritise being liked or gaining quick approval, pause and ask yourself: *Will this decision help me build the long-term respect of my team?* Because respect, not approval, is the foundation of great leadership.

One of the key themes we discussed in Rule #2 was about having tough conversations – conversations that many managers avoid for fear of being disliked (see page 37). But here's the thing: those difficult conversations are essential for building respect. When you address issues head-on, even if it's uncomfortable, your team recognises your willingness to tackle problems rather than sweep them under the rug. They may not *like* it in the moment, but they'll *respect* you for it in the long run.

Difficult conversations don't just solve immediate problems – they build a foundation of respect, which is far more valuable than short-term approval.

SETTING BOUNDARIES: THE KEY TO EARNING RESPECT

This is where boundaries come into play. You may have heard a thousand times that 'you need clear boundaries', but it's easy to gloss over the importance of this when you're trying to please everyone around you. The moment I started setting boundaries, everything changed. I stopped thinking of boundaries as a rigid checklist or a way to shut people out. Instead, I reframed them as a way to prioritise what mattered most. I realised that saying yes to everything wasn't helping anyone in the long term – not my team, not the business, and definitely not me. Boundaries weren't about being unapproachable; they were about being intentional.

For me, it started with pausing before I said yes. Instead of immediately agreeing to every request, I began asking myself a few key questions:

- Does this align with my role and responsibilities?

- Do I have the capacity to take this on without compromising other priorities?

- Am I the best person to handle this or is this something my team can take ownership of?

- What's the impact of saying yes – and what's the cost?

These questions acted as a mental filter. They forced me to consider the bigger picture instead of reacting emotionally or out of habit. Over time, this pause became second nature. I found that by setting clear expectations my team saw me as a stronger, more focused leader.

Boundaries require us to be thoughtful about saying yes. They're a way to protect your time and energy so you can show up fully for the things that matter most. Here are the key boundaries that every manager needs to set:

Time boundaries

As a manager, your time is one of your most valuable resources. Yet, without clear time boundaries, it's easy to become consumed by endless tasks and demands. By setting strict time limits around your working time, you ensure that you not only protect your own productivity, but also model healthy work habits for your team. Time boundaries are essential for avoiding burnout and maintaining a sustainable pace of work.

- **Stop replying to team messages outside of work hours** – this sets the expectation that your time is valuable and that work can wait.

  If you work flexibly and choose to respond at non-standard hours, make it clear that this is for your own schedule, not because you expect an immediate reply. You can do this by:

  - Adding a note in your email signature explaining your working style.

  - Scheduling emails to be sent during regular work hours instead of when you write them.

  Clarity prevents miscommunication and helps set healthy boundaries for everyone.

- **When you're on a break – whether it's lunch or a holiday – be fully on the break.** Your team will learn to respect your need for downtime and, in turn, value their own.

- **Evaluate every meeting invite with scrutiny.** Is it necessary? Could the same thing be achieved via email? Protect your time fiercely because it's your most valuable resource.

Energy boundaries

Your mental energy is as finite as your time and, without boundaries, you can find yourself drained before the work-day is even over. Energy boundaries help you focus on what really matters, ensuring that you aren't bogged down by drama or tasks that aren't aligned with your strengths – or your team's. Protecting your energy enables you to lead with clarity and composure.

- **Deal with workplace issues factually, without letting yourself be dragged into unnecessary drama.** We need to stay focused on solutions while still showing compassion. When conversations become overly emotional, I redirect them by acknowledging the feelings involved and then shifting the focus to actionable steps. For example, I might say: 'I can see how frustrating this must be – let's talk about what we can do to address it and move forward.' This approach ensures that you're empathetic without letting emotions derail progress.

- **Don't take on tasks that don't align with yours, or your team's, strengths.** Protecting your energy means knowing when to push back, not just for yourself but for your team as well. If a task doesn't fit within your team's expertise or capacity, it's okay to say no or delegate it elsewhere. For example, if an additional project is assigned, ask yourself: *Is this something that aligns with our team's goals? Do we have the bandwidth to do it well?* Saying no on behalf of your team is one of the most powerful ways to protect their time, energy and morale. It's not about avoiding responsibility – it's about ensuring your team has the space to excel at the work that truly matters. And when your team is focused and working within their strengths, you, as a manager, avoid burnout, decision fatigue, and the stress of constantly firefighting misaligned tasks.

- **Prioritise work that adds value, aligns with your goals and eliminates redundancy.** Take the time to evaluate workflows and look for inefficiencies that might be draining your team's energy. Are there reports or meetings that no longer serve a purpose? Can repetitive tasks be streamlined, automated or consolidated? By actively reducing redundancy, you not only protect your team's mental energy, but also create space for them to focus on impactful, strategic work. This sends a clear message that their time is valued and their contributions matter. And when your team is working efficiently, it protects your energy as a manager – freeing you from constant oversight, reducing unnecessary decision-making, and allowing you to focus on higher-level leadership priorities.

Pace boundaries

In today's mega-fast work environment, it's easy to feel swept up in the urgency of everything. But the greatest leaders know this: not every task requires your immediate attention, and not every message needs to be read and responded to within one minute.

- **Set expectations around response times.** Clearly communicating your boundaries helps you and your team align on what 'urgent' truly means. For example, you might say, 'I'll respond to non-urgent emails within 24 hours, but if something is time-sensitive, flag it with "urgent" in the subject line or contact me directly.' This not only manages others' expectations, but also creates psychological safety for your team to do the same.

- **Distinguish between urgent and important work.** One of the most effective tools for this is the Eisenhower Matrix, which categorises tasks into four quadrants: urgent and important, important but not urgent, urgent but not important, and neither urgent nor important. For example:

  1. **Urgent and important:** A critical client presentation happening in two hours.

  2. **Important but not urgent:** Building a long-term strategy for your team.

  3. **Urgent but not important:** Replying to non-essential emails or attending low-value meetings.

  4. **Neither urgent nor important:** Mindlessly scrolling social media during work hours (guilty).

  Focusing your energy on tasks in the 'important but not urgent' category allows you to invest in long-term goals while reducing last-minute scrambling.

- **Communicate your priorities to the team.** Generally at work, everyone's priorities will be vastly different, so when communicating those priorities, transparency is key. Start by acknowledging their request, then explain your current focus and timeline. For example: 'I understand this feels pressing, and I want to give it the attention it deserves. At the moment, I'm focused on [specific high-priority task or goal], which aligns with [broader business goal]. Could we discuss a realistic timeline for this request so I can ensure it gets done well?'

> ## PRACTICAL STEPS TO REDUCE CONSTANT INTERRUPTIONS
>
> 1. **Schedule time for emails.** Check emails at set intervals – such as twice a day – rather than constantly refreshing your inbox. (This one is tough to keep the discipline around – it's taken me a good few years to do it fully, but now I'm there it really is so powerful.)
>
> 2. **Turn off notifications.** Disabling alerts prevents minor distractions from derailing your focus. Nothing is urgent enough to steal your immediate attention.
>
> 3. **Introduce time blocks for high-impact tasks.** Dedicate uninterrupted blocks of time to your most meaningful work, and communicate these focus periods to your team.

The ability to set pace boundaries, prioritise effectively and communicate transparently not only boosts productivity, but also establishes you as a thoughtful, respected leader.

The Courage to Disappoint

Being a manager means you will inevitably disappoint people at times. You won't be able to say yes to every request, you'll have to deliver tough feedback and there will be moments when your team might not like your decisions. But that's okay. It's essential we start feeling a little more at ease knowing we can't please everyone, and we may have to even disappoint people at times.

We've already explored how you can't lead by trying to be liked by everyone, but the courage to be the person who makes the difficult decisions, even when they're unpopular, is a fundamental aspect of leadership. And the reality is, if you're not upsetting someone from time to time, you're probably avoiding the tough choices that drive progress and balance the needs of the team and the organisation.

The key is to ask yourself: *Am I staying true to my values, my goals and the best interests of my team?* If the answer is yes, then it's okay if not everyone agrees with you. Leadership isn't about pleasing everyone; it's about making decisions that move the team forward, even if they're uncomfortable in the moment.

So, let's wrap up: what does it mean to lead with respect over approval? It means:

- making decisions that protect your energy and focus, even when they're not popular

- setting boundaries and sticking to them, so you can lead sustainably

- recognising that being liked is nice, but being respected and effective is far more kind and valuable in the long run

Managers who focus on short-term approval often find themselves burned out, overcommitted and unable to lead effectively. People-pleasing doesn't just exhaust you – it distracts you and your team from achieving your goals. By setting boundaries, saying no when needed and prioritising respect, you create a more focused, productive environment that drives meaningful results.

What to Do When You're Managing a People-Pleaser

As managers, it's also important to spot people-pleasing behaviours in your team. You might notice a team member who struggles to say no, overcommits to tasks, stays late to redo work unnecessarily or agrees with everything in meetings to avoid conflict. While their intentions might come from a good place, these behaviours can lead to burnout, resentment and, ultimately, reduced performance.

So, what can you do to help a people-pleaser thrive without falling into the trap of overextending themselves? Here are some practical strategies:

1. **Encourage open conversations about workload.**
   Create a safe space for team members to share when they feel overwhelmed. Ask specific questions like, 'How are you finding your current workload?' or 'Do you feel you have the capacity to take this on?' This can help uncover hidden pressures they might not vocalise otherwise.

2. **Help them set boundaries.** Coach them on how to pause before saying yes to every request. Teach them to assess tasks by asking themselves questions like:

   - Does this align with my priorities?

   - Do I have the capacity to do this well?

   - Is this something I need to handle personally, or can I delegate or share it?

By reinforcing that saying no is a sign of strength, not weakness, you empower them to manage their time and energy better.

3. **Model healthy boundaries.** Our team will mirror the behaviours they see in their leader. If you're constantly overcommitting or never saying no, they're likely to do the same. Demonstrate what healthy boundaries look like by protecting your own time, delegating effectively and being transparent about your priorities.

4. **Acknowledge their efforts without reinforcing overextension.** When giving feedback, avoid praising behaviours like working overtime or taking on too much, as this can unintentionally encourage them to keep overextending. Instead, celebrate the quality of their work and their ability to prioritise effectively.

When you personally prioritise respect over approval, you set the tone for your team to do the same. By coaching people-pleasers to say no when needed and focus on what matters, you protect them from burnout and create a stronger, more sustainable work culture.

And as you build that culture of respect, you'll notice something remarkable: you become not just a manager, but a leader who inspires confidence, delivers results and creates a team that thrives – all without chasing the fleeting approval.

People-pleasing might feel like the easiest path to harmony, but it often leads to burnout, resentment and ineffective leadership. And, as managers, we must recognise and overcome people-pleasing tendencies in ourselves and our teams, coaching others to prioritise what matters and protect their energy. By shifting our focus from short-term approval to lasting respect, we create a culture of trust, accountability and sustainable success – for ourselves, our teams and the organisation.

But setting boundaries and making tough calls is only part of the equation – who you surround yourself with matters just as much. The right people will challenge, support, and elevate you as a leader.

Surround Yourself with Great People

No matter how strong-minded we become in leadership, there will always be moments – sometimes days or even weeks – filled with doubt, frustration and uncertainty about the path we're on. And let me be real for a second: if you're not experiencing this every now and then, you've likely stopped learning, and that's a red flag in itself. It's those moments of self-doubt and the willingness to admit that we don't have all the answers that keep us growing.

My biggest wins in leadership have come from my lowest points, moments when I've had to stop because the doubt is so strong, and ask myself, *What's the lesson in this?* And that's when reaching out to others has made all the difference. The mentors I have around me help me hit pause and regroup with a new perspective. That's when I come out the other side even stronger. Finding mentors and strong influences – both within and outside the company I'm working in – has been transformative for my career. When you're questioning your abilities or feeling unsure about your next move, having the right people to lean on is pivotal. Your network acts as your anchor and, in times of uncertainty, the people around you will either lift you up or pull you down, which is why it is so important to surround yourself well.

I get messages almost daily asking, 'But how do I find a mentor?' Maybe you've already reached out to people inside or outside your organisation and been met with rejection or silence, or maybe you're working from home, where building those connections feels even harder. It's easy to feel stuck when opportunities for in-person networking or casual conversations are limited.

But here's the thing: my first mentors didn't even know my name. I never met them, and I never had to ask for permission to learn and grow from their insights, yet they were some of the most impactful mentors I've ever had. And the best part? You can find mentors like these in seconds, no matter where you work.

Curate Your Feed, Control Your Space

It's time to have a serious chat about your digital environment. We've all heard the quote, 'You are the average of the five people you spend the most time with.' But Jim Rohn said that over ten years ago. And today, the average British adult spends *nearly SEVEN hours a day on their phone*. That means your digital distractions – social media, news apps, streaming platforms – are now the people you 'spend the most time with'.

In my early twenties, my social media feed was making me miserable. I was following influencers, models and celebrities who painted a picture of perfection that left me feeling deeply insecure about the way I looked, my relationships and my career. I was regularly comparing myself to a Kardashian buying their third house, a travel influencer going on their sixth holiday that year or a Victoria's Secret model taking a glam mirror selfie. One particularly sad day when I'd started to despise all the clothes in my wardrobe and how they looked on my body, I decided enough was enough. I unfollowed all the accounts that were making me question my self-worth. Gone were the celebrities, the trust fund kids and the beauty queens. I needed to change my internal monologue and use my social media feeds to help me.

Once I finished the unfollowing, I took it a step further. I thought, hey, what if I actively filled my feed with accounts that inspired me? Not just in looks, but in mindset, leadership, philosophy and personal growth? I started clicking through hashtags like 'personal development' and 'leadership' to find role models I could aspire to be like and who could help inspire me during my toughest times.

I'll never have an exact statistic or measure to know how much impact this truly had on me, but all I know is, a short while after curating my feed, I:

- felt more energised and clearer about my career direction

- swapped scrolling for reading before bed

- left a relationship I'd been in for far too long that wasn't working

- started actually going to the gym and committing to exercise, which now, six years later, is a huge part of my life

- developed a 10x healthier relationship with food

Over time, these habits have compounded into me being the happiest, healthiest and most successful version of me I can be right now.

And the great news is you can do this exact same thing – it costs nothing and you don't even have to move from your sofa to do it. You can take back control over who and what you let influence you. Your phone is your gateway to a curated world, and you get to decide exactly what's inside it. If you're intentional about what you consume, your digital world can be a space that uplifts, motivates and guides you. Here's all you need to do:

- **Unfollow accounts that make you feel like you're not enough.** These could be influencers whose posts make you question your self-worth or celebrities who paint unrealistic pictures of life and unrealistic ideals of success.

- **Follow leaders, thinkers and influencers who share valuable insights, genuine stories and advice that adds to your journey.** This doesn't have to mean the hustle crypto bros, just people who are authentic about their world and stories.

- **Engage with content that promotes growth, learning and mindfulness.** Positive news platforms, body positivity advocates and accounts focused on mental health can create a huge mindset shift over time.

A study by the Royal Society for Public Health surveyed 1,479 people aged 14–24, asking them to score popular apps on issues such as anxiety, depression, loneliness, bullying and body image. Instagram was ranked as the worst social media platform for mental health overall, with 70 per cent of users reporting a negative effect on their self-image.

TikTok, for example, is rapidly becoming a dominant force in social media, further blurring the lines between entertainment and potential mental health risks.

You could choose to ditch platforms like Instagram or TikTok altogether, but I think that by curating your feed, you can transform your experience on these platforms, and the algorithm will quickly take note too. Here are a few types of accounts that can be especially valuable for us managers:

- **Leadership and management experts.** Following thought leaders like Adam Grant, Brené Brown and Liz Wiseman can offer actionable tips and fresh perspectives on leadership. These accounts share guidance that encourage growth, and their content is like having a pocket-sized mentor reminding you to lead with empathy, purpose and strategy.

- **Finance and investment advisers.** Money management is a core skill for any professional, and learning from finance experts can make a huge difference. Accounts like @girlsthatinvest and @abigailrosefoster are fantastic resources that provide digestible advice on managing personal finances and investments. For me, they've been game-changing in helping me feel more in control of my money, approach decisions with confidence and understand how financial literacy connects to professional success.

- **Positive news platforms.** Mainstream media often leans into anxiety-inducing headlines, which can leave us feeling drained. Good-news platforms, like @thehappynewspaper, share uplifting and inspiring stories that help shift your mindset. These accounts remind us that there's still so much good happening in the world, which can help managers stay optimistic and foster a positive attitude that's contagious to their teams.

- **Mindfulness and mental health advocates.** Stress is inevitable in management, but mindfulness can be a powerful tool to combat it. Following accounts focused on mindfulness and mental health can provide daily tips to stay present, reduce anxiety and approach challenges calmly. These accounts encourage practices that help managers stay grounded during high-pressure moments, which in turn benefits the entire team. A fave of mine is @ wearefeelgoodclub.

- **Philosophy.** For me, this looked like following accounts focused on Stoicism, like @dailystoic. These accounts share insights that help us keep a level head, especially in high-stress moments. Stoic principles, for example, remind us to focus only on what we can control, which can be incredibly grounding in leadership. Following philosophy accounts can help you approach challenges with a clearer mindset, stay resilient and make decisions with greater wisdom. They provide a daily reminder for me to lead with intention and to see obstacles as opportunities for growth.

Intentional social media choices enable us to hand-curate a digital environment that truly supports our goals. It's a small step, yet with powerful compounding results that help shape our mindset. You have the ability to build a space filled with people who inspire you, keep you focused and help you stay on track.

But while digital mentors can offer guidance from afar, there's still immense value in building real-world connections. A few years after curating my feed, I experienced first-hand the transformative impact of in-person mentors and it truly accelerated my growth. These mentors can provide tailored advice based on our unique challenges and setbacks, seeing our journey up close and offering insights that resonate on a deeper level.

Real-Life Mentors

As important as your digital mentors are, real-life connections are essential. Finding mentors and allies in your physical space can profoundly affect your confidence, decision-making and resilience as a leader. I've had several mentors who, each in their own way, helped shape who I am as a leader today.

When I first became a manager, I felt I was in over my head. At the time, I had great admiration for Emma – I've changed her name here, but she was a senior leader in a different department to me at work, who always seemed calm, composed and decisive, especially in meetings that I found super intimidating. She had this way of listening intently and asking just the right questions that encouraged others to reflect. Emma's presence particularly struck me during a meeting where we faced a complicated disagreement that made me feel overwhelmed. Instead of quickly offering a solution, she asked each person involved to share their perspective, one by one. Watching her handle the situation with so much patience and empathy made me realise how powerful it was to lead with both clarity and care.

I knew I could learn a lot from Emma, but approaching her felt daunting. After giving it some thought, I sent her an email with a clear and simple request:

Subject: Chat request

Hi Emma,

I hope you're well. I wanted to reach out because I've really admired your leadership approach in meetings, especially the way you handled that complex situation in the meeting yesterday with such clarity and empathy. I'd love to learn from your experience and wondered if you'd be open to a quick coffee sometime. I have some questions that I could do with your advice on, and I'd value anything you could share to help me on my journey.

Thank you for considering, and no pressure at all if your schedule doesn't allow.

Thanks so much,

Heather

She graciously agreed, and that coffee turned into monthly check-ins. Emma's insights helped me navigate the early challenges I faced as a new manager, and her guidance changed my perspective on lots of common management issues I'd been having. Over time, I found myself modelling some of her techniques, especially in situations where tensions ran high. Emma's mentorship taught me the value of patience and reflection.

This is how simple a mentorship request can be. It doesn't need to be someone super unreachable from a famous organisation in a different country to yours; it can just be someone with a certain set of skills that you particularly admire in your own company. I know over the months Emma learned a good few things from me too, and it was great to have a sounding board for my issues.

BUILDING A SOLID NETWORK

Having mentors within your organisation is invaluable, but it's equally important to build a network beyond your immediate environment.

> *External mentors bring fresh perspectives and insights that can shift how you view challenges, providing new ideas and solutions that might not emerge within your usual circles.*

For me, LinkedIn became the powerful tool I used to build that external network. Early on, while I was still an employee at a small company in London, I started sharing small glimpses into my day-to-day work life on LinkedIn. I didn't have any grand achievements to share, it was usually just behind-the-scenes moments, lessons learned and observations about leadership and my work, but this simple act of sharing helped me reflect on my experiences and articulate them well. Those posts *eventually* became the foundations for this book, but before that, they began my journey of building connections with others who shared similar goals and challenges.

Over time, this network became a lifeline, introducing me to people I would never have met otherwise and even leading me to some of those mentors who were so important in shaping my growth. When I'd go to industry conferences, it meant I had already connected with people and could deepen those connections, instead of going into scary rooms and having to introduce myself without knowing anyone. These connections still benefit me today – they're a source of support, insight and camaraderie that I lean on when work feels isolating.

For managers, this kind of external support network is crucial. I think we've all come to believe that LinkedIn is only for self-employed people, sales people or recruiters. But it is a social media platform just like any other; it's just one that encourages sharing about work learnings and challenges, rather than our personal lives.

When you're only talking to your team or senior leaders at work, it can feel a little isolating. But having others who understand these hurdles and share similar fears and goals creates a real sense of community. You realise you're not the only one facing these pressures, and that sense of solidarity can make the tough moments feel more manageable.

If you're not yet building an external network, LinkedIn is a fab place to start. It takes a little courage to put yourself out there, but if you're clear about why you want to connect, many leaders and peers are open to genuine conversations. And remember, mentorship is a two-way street. By offering mentorship to others, you not only help them, but also clarify your own perspectives, gain empathy and become a more grounded leader in the process.

A couple of years after Emma had left our team, I found myself ready to tackle a new level of leadership, but was unsure who to turn to for advice. I'd recently been promoted into the director of operations role, and I'd made external contact on LinkedIn with a great chief operating officer (COO) in our industry (but at a different company) called Martin. Martin had experience running businesses and navigating high-stakes challenges. When I'd first seen his content, I was just admiring from afar, watching all the brilliant work he was doing with his team, so I reached out and asked if I could take him for coffee next time I was in London.

He agreed, and his advice in that session alone was invaluable. We didn't meet frequently – he was more of a mentor from afar who I exchanged WhatsApps with here and there – but, when we spoke, I found that his outside perspective brought a really refreshing sense of clarity. Because he wasn't tangled in my day-to-day challenges, he could see things I couldn't. Martin encouraged me to be bolder, challenged my thinking, got me to take ownership of my own problems (instead of blaming others) and ultimately helped me build the resilience to withstand setbacks.

Approaching someone like Martin online can feel intimidating, but most people are willing to help if they feel their experience could be valuable. Here's a simple guide on how to ask someone for mentorship:

1. **Observe their work or approach and be *specific* about why you admire them.**

2. **Reach out with a clear, concise request.** Mention what you appreciate about them, and ask for a brief coffee or meeting.

3. **Be clear and respectful of their time.** Let them know that you're not expecting a long-term commitment, but would simply value their advice.

Here's a script you can adapt (I'd add a bit of your personality to it):

> **Subject: Seeking guidance on [specific topic]**
>
> Hi [Name],
>
> I hope this message finds you well! I've been following your work and can't help but admire how brilliantly you [mention specific skill or quality you admire]. It's so inspiring to see how you approach [specific area of expertise], and I'd love to learn from your insights.
>
> I'm currently working on developing similar skills and thought I'd reach out to see if you might be open to a quick coffee or Zoom chat sometime. I'd be so grateful for even 20 minutes of your time to ask you some questions and hear your perspective. Of course, I completely understand if things are too busy on your end right now.
>
> Thank you so much for considering this – it means a lot to me.
>
> Warm regards,
>
> [Your name]

Don't be disheartened if it takes many, many emails before you get a response (remember the rejection log from Rule #5 – see page 86). I probably reached out to 15 other potential mentors before Martin and got no response. Rejection isn't a reflection of your worth – it's a step on the path to finding the right people who truly resonate with your journey. Every 'no' gets you closer to the mentor who's meant to help you grow. Keep reaching out; it only takes one 'yes' to make a really powerful impact.

If you feel like you're asking for something in exchange for nothing, remember this: mentorship is often about connection, not just transaction. When you approach someone with curiosity and a genuine appreciation for their work, you're not just asking for their time – you're recognising their expertise and inviting them to share what they're passionate about. Many people enjoy giving back and sharing their knowledge, especially when approached with sincerity.

To make the conversation feel more balanced, think about what you can bring to the table. Maybe it's sharing how their work has impacted you, offering to assist with something small or simply showing that you're eager to apply what you learn from them. Demonstrating that you value their time and are committed to taking action based on their advice can go a long way. So, don't let that feeling hold you back.

Mentors within your company can help you navigate your specific culture, offering guidance on effective communication with different teams and advice on internal processes. External mentors, on the other hand, bring an unbiased view – they aren't clouded by office politics or departmental challenges and bring fresh eyes to your situation, which can make all the difference.

Paid mentorship

During one of my most challenging transitions as a manager, I reached out to a third kind of mentor: an executive leadership coach. I was still in my operations director role, but had moved into the corporate world at this point, and although I was having great results on the outside, inside I was struggling to adapt, so I requested to use the company training budget to invest in my development with an external coach. They said yes, and I so reached out to Anna. Anna was the first paid mentor I'd worked with and she was unlike any other mentor I'd had. Anna pushed me hard and didn't sugar-coat feedback. She challenged me to question my assumptions, helped me identify my blind spots and showed me the value of being reflective rather than reactive.

Investing in paid mentorship helped me to feel as though it was a commitment to serious, intentional growth. When you invest in a mentor, you're accessing years of specialised experience and receiving undivided attention tailored to your unique journey. Paid mentors hold you to a high standard and offer accountability that goes beyond casual guidance. By utilising your company's training budget to seek this kind of specialised support, you're taking ownership of your growth while making use of existing resources designed to help you excel. Use something like this to ask for access to the company's training budget:

Subject: Request for training budget approval
Hi [Manager's name],
I hope you're well. I've been reflecting on ways to further develop my skills and make a greater impact in my role, and I've identified an opportunity that I believe would be a great fit.

There's a mentor I'd like to work with who specialises in [specific area: for example, leadership development, strategic thinking, etc.], and their guidance could help me [specific outcome: for example, improve my ability to manage complex projects, develop stronger leadership skills, etc.]. This mentorship would provide tailored, one-on-one support, offering actionable strategies and accountability to help me grow in areas directly tied to my work.

I'd like to explore the possibility of utilising our training budget for this purpose. The investment would not only support my personal development, but also enhance my ability to contribute to [specific team or company goals: for example, increasing productivity, improving team collaboration, etc.].

[Now provide additional details about the mentorship programme, including cost, expected outcomes, etc.]

Thank you for considering this request. I really value the support and investment the company puts into our growth, and I'm excited about the opportunity to take this next step. I'd love to discuss this further and answer any questions you might have.

Best regards,

[Your name]

Starting out as a manager can feel like being handed the reins without a map. But a mentor can help in providing that map, offering confidence and direction. A five-year study by Gartner involving 1,000 employees revealed that mentees are promoted five times more often than those not in a mentoring relationship. Additionally, retention rates were higher for both mentees and mentors compared to those not participating in such programmes. This shows us the profound impact mentorship can have on our career advancement and stability. Whether formal or informal, a mentoring relationship can accelerate your development in ways no course or textbook ever could.

Each of my mentors has brought something unique to my development. With my needs changing throughout the years, different mentors came into play at different times and guided me through unique phases of my journey, pushing me towards the leader I am today.

My story isn't unique. Many leaders I know have found mentors along the way who guided and challenged them. Whether you're a new manager or not, there is a huge untapped opportunity for you in continually seeking out the people – whether in your company or outside of it – who align with your values, have navigated the kinds of challenges you're facing and are willing to guide you.

Let's Round Up

Surrounding yourself with the right 'people' – both online and in real life – makes all the difference in Your Boss Era. When you're intentional about curating your digital environment, you're choosing influences that lift you up and keep you focused. And, in the real world, having mentors to guide you through challenges brings a level of support and perspective that's hard to match. Whether it's reaching out on LinkedIn, finding someone in your company or even investing in a coach, mentors come in all shapes and sizes and bring something unique to your journey.

But building a solid network can't end with us pulling these people around us, it's also about showing up for others as the authentic person we are too. Authenticity in leadership is powerful because it builds trust, inspires others and creates a genuine connection with your team. When you lead as your true self, people feel it and they're more likely to believe in you, support you, show up for you and open up with their own ideas and perspectives. So, in the next chapter, let's dive into what it means to show up authentically and why it's one of the most powerful things you can do as a leader.

Show Up as Your Whole Self

Picture this: 21-year-old Heather, freshly promoted to her first full-time management role at Harrods, standing nervously on the shop floor. My team was older, more experienced and carried themselves with a polish I could only hope to fake. The weight of the environment was immense: luxurious displays, customers with sky-high expectations and a culture steeped in tradition. I was desperate to prove I belonged, but every instinct told me to be someone I wasn't.

The whispers of imposter syndrome were loud: *Dress the part. Speak the part. Don't let them see your inexperience.* And so, I did what most of us are conditioned to do – I conformed. My Northern accent softened, my personality muted and I avoided challenging the status quo, fearing that speaking up might expose me as 'too young' or 'not professional enough'.

I remember one particular instance vividly. A customer had an issue with a return, a situation where the policy was clearly on their side, but the manager on duty dismissed them brusquely, insisting it wasn't worth the hassle. Deep down, I knew it wasn't the right call. It absolutely didn't align with how I believed customers should be treated or the values of the business, but I stayed quiet. I told myself, *They know better than I do*, even though it didn't sit well with me. I nodded along, feeling complicit and small, but too afraid to challenge the decision or suggest an alternative.

It wasn't just Harrods. These patterns had been ingrained long before I set foot on that shop floor. The pressure to conform is evolutionary. Our brains are wired to prioritise belonging. Thousands of years ago, fitting into a group was essential for survival – being different could mean being left behind or excluded. Even now, our instincts tell us that standing out can feel unsafe, especially in high-stakes environments like the workplace.

This is why we often default to the 'façade of conformity'. In a 2024 article, 'Invisible mending: The silent struggle of conforming at work,' *Psychology Today* explains how many people suppress their true values or opinions to fit in with workplace norms. It discusses how employees often engage in 'invisible mending', subtly altering their behaviour and suppressing their true selves to align with workplace norms, which can lead to significant psychological stress and identity conflict.

It's not just exhausting for individuals, but it's detrimental to organisations, too. Suppressing diverse perspectives and ideas is like tying one hand behind your back and expecting yourself and your team to perform at full capacity.

These evolutionary instincts are reinforced by societal conditioning. From the moment we enter school, we're taught to fit in: *Sit up straight. Follow the rules. Put your hand up before you speak.* These lessons aren't necessarily bad ones, but they instil a subtle message: blending in is safer than standing out. Creativity, curiosity and individuality are often sidelined in favour of compliance and uniformity.

Take school uniforms as an example. While they may teach discipline, they also reinforce the idea that being 'good' or 'successful' means looking like everyone else. By extension, we aim to fit in with our actions too. This conditioning doesn't stop when we leave school – it follows us into adulthood, shaping how we think professionalism should look and feel.

As we grow older, the pressure to conform is amplified by the media. Leaders in films, TV shows and adverts are almost always depicted as immaculate and unshakeable – calm, perfectly dressed and rarely emotional. These portrayals create a blueprint for what we believe leadership should look like, even if it feels completely at odds with who we are.

And then there's social media. Platforms like Instagram fuel a culture of perfection, flooding us with images of 'ideal' lives, flawless careers and polished personalities. It's no wonder we feel like we need to mould ourselves into someone else's idea of 'success'.

I remember feeling this acutely in the early days. Every decision, every interaction felt like a performance. And while I thought I was doing what was necessary to succeed, by pretending to be something I'm not, I was actually holding myself, and my team, back.

As the years rolled on, team members with diverse perspectives came and went. I moved companies and cities, and, slowly, I started to learn that no one wins when we suppress our individuality. One moment stands out vividly.

I was working in a new role, managing a small but ambitious team. Among them was a new manager called Amara, a brilliant project manager who wasn't afraid to bring her whole self to work. Amara's ideas were bold, her approach unconventional and she never hesitated to share insights rooted in her unique perspectives on the world. At first, I wasn't sure how her style would sit within the wider team – it was so different to the traditional, buttoned-up professionalism I'd been taught to value.

But something unexpected happened. Amara's authenticity became a catalyst for the team. Her openness encouraged others to speak up, offer ideas they might have kept to themselves and challenge old ways of working. It wasn't always smooth sailing – her approach often sparked debate – but the team's output became stronger, more creative and undeniably better.

Watching Amara, I realised something crucial: leadership can't be about fitting into an idealised mould; it's about showing up as yourself and inspiring others to do the same. It became clear that when we embrace individuality, we unlock untapped potential in our teams.

This was a turning point for me, where I truly understood that authenticity is the bedrock of great leadership. The more I leaned into it, the more I saw my teams flourish. Authenticity became my compass – a way to build trust, encourage innovation and lead with genuine connection.

Harvard Business School highlights research showing that authentic leadership really does make a difference. A study in the *Leadership & Organization Development Journal* found that when employees see their leaders as authentic, it's the biggest factor in how satisfied they feel at work, how committed they are to the organisation and even how happy they are in their roles.

A standout example of authentic leadership is Ursula Burns, former CEO of Xerox and the first Black woman to lead a Fortune 500 company. Burns navigated 2009 corporate America, where 'diversity' existed as a buzzword more than a reality. Through relentless hard work and determination, she rose to the top, unapologetically embracing her humble beginnings and addressing the challenges she faced as a woman of colour in a predominantly white, male-dominated environment.

Burns once said, 'I realised I was more convincing to myself and to the people who were listening when I actually said what I thought, versus what I thought people wanted to hear me say.' Her commitment to being her true self earned her the trust of her employees and peers.

One of her first bold moves was to establish a diversity advisory board at Xerox, tasked with creating real pathways for underrepresented groups to enter and advance within the company. Burns also introduced targeted leadership programmes to ensure that women and minorities had opportunities for mentorship, skill-building and promotion into senior roles.

She faced resistance from colleagues who questioned whether her initiatives were necessary and feared they might disrupt hierarchies. Others doubted whether diverse leadership could ever deliver the same results as traditional models. Still, Burns pressed on. Amid big challenge, she refused to shy away from the difficult conversations. And her commitment paid off. Xerox became a trailblazer in corporate diversity, with women and minorities holding over 40 per cent of senior management positions during her tenure. Burns also extended her focus externally, pushing for supplier diversity by ensuring Xerox partnered with minority- and women-owned businesses. These movements generated tangible results for the company and its stakeholders, and drove economic growth in underrepresented communities while building stronger supplier relationships.

On top of that, she had tapped into a wider range of perspectives in the team at Xerox, which fuelled creativity, improved decision-making and ultimately strengthened Xerox's reputation as an innovative, forward-thinking organisation.

The reason I look up to Burns so much is because she turned the very things that made her not fit the mould in corporate America – her background and her identity – into her greatest strengths. She shined a light on them and leaned even further into the parts that made her so special and unique. When I started my career, I often found myself hiding the parts of me that I didn't think would fit into the corporate mould. My accent, my unconventional ideas, even the way I approached conversations – I tried to smooth them out, thinking that blending in was the only way to succeed. Burns did the opposite and, to me, her leadership became proof that when you embrace who you truly are and push back against the outdated norms, you can achieve real results in yourself and your teams.

Psychological research published in the *Journal of Business Ethics* found a strong link between authentic leadership and employee engagement. Teams led by authentic leaders feel more valued and engaged, and are ultimately more productive. Being authentic is brave, especially in a world that rewards conformity. But the rewards are worth it. As a leader, you have the power to set the tone. When you commit to authenticity, you give your team permission to do the same. Together, you can create an environment where trust, creativity and connection thrive.

It's not easy. I know that from my time at Harrods. But I also know that the opportunity for managers who are willing to be bold, break free from the mould and lead authentically has never been greater. In a world tired of cookie-cutter professionals and corporate clichés, the leaders who stand out are the ones who dare to show up as their true selves.

Think about the CEO you admire most, the one whose leadership you look up to – they weren't born into their role with all the answers. Once upon a time, they were a new manager too, battling imposter syndrome and wondering if they were good enough. The difference? They dared to push for something greater. They took risks, made mistakes and leaned into the discomfort of standing out instead of blending in.

Authenticity sets you apart, makes you relatable, builds trust and connection, and inspires loyalty from everyone around you. And that kind of culture is truly special because it creates an environment where people feel safe to speak up, share ideas and be themselves.

In a workplace like that, innovation thrives, communication is honest and people feel genuinely valued for who they are, not just what they do. Teams become more resilient, collaboration improves and employees are more engaged and committed. It's the kind of culture where people want to show up not because they have to, but because they feel they belong.

So, what do we actually mean when we talk about 'being an authentic leader'? In the next section, we're going to break it down. With practical examples and actionable insights, we'll explore what authenticity looks like in leadership – and how you can make it a part of Your Boss Era too.

What Is 'Authenticity' Anyway?

The definition of authenticity is the quality of being genuine, true to one's values and consistent in actions, regardless of external pressures or expectations. It involves showing up as

When you embrace who you are, quirks and all, you send a powerful message to your team: 'You can be real here.'

your true self, rather than conforming to societal or organisational norms, and acting in alignment with your beliefs, values and personality.

An authentic leader acknowledges their strengths and weaknesses, shows vulnerability when appropriate and, in turn, creates an environment where others feel safe to do the same. As Brené Brown, a prominent researcher on vulnerability and authenticity, puts it: 'Authenticity is the daily practice of letting go of who we think we're supposed to be and embracing who we are.'

Reflecting on the early years of my career, I realise I wasn't leading at all; I was performing. And my eagerness to 'fit in' was holding me back. By conforming to idealised leadership archetypes, I was unintentionally signalling to my team that they needed to do the same. By staying silent, I was failing my team and the people who relied on me.

Over time, I began experimenting with showing up more authentically. It started small: voicing my honest opinions in meetings, even when my heart was pounding, and letting my Northern accent shine through instead of masking it. But authenticity is about more than just how you sound in a meeting; it's about letting people see the person behind the role.

For years, I kept my personal life tucked away at work. I thought it was more 'professional' to separate the two. I avoided talking about my family, where I was from or even who I went home to at the end of the day. Being gay, I'd always been wary of how people might react at work if I mentioned my female partner. I told myself it wasn't relevant to my job, but, deep down, I worried about how I'd be perceived. Would I be seen as 'different'? Too personal? Too much? What if I offended someone?

Then, one day, during a team lunch, someone casually asked about my weekend. I paused for a second, feeling that familiar hesitation, before I decided to answer honestly. I told them I'd spent Sunday with my girlfriend, going for a walk and planning a trip we'd been excited about for ages. The room was quiet for a moment, and I braced myself, but then someone smiled and said, 'That sounds amazing – where are you going?' The conversation moved on, but something shifted for me in that moment. I realised how much of myself I'd been holding back out of fear, and just how unnecessary that fear really was.

From then on, I started opening up more – not just about my weekends or my relationship, but about who I was as a person. I shared stories about growing up in a small Northern town, helping my grandad with his allotment and watching my mum work tirelessly building her business. And the more I shared, the more my team responded. They started opening up about their own lives, their challenges, their quirks. We built a deeper connection, one that went beyond titles and job descriptions.

Looking back, I see now that my need to seem 'professional' had held me back from forming those connections for years. I'd wanted to appear polished and capable – everything I thought a leader should be. But that façade wasn't helping anyone. The more I leaned into who I really was, the more my team trusted me.

And the more I leaned into who I really was, the more I noticed a shift. First, in myself and how I felt walking into work each morning. Instead of dreading the day ahead or questioning if I was good enough, I started to feel powerful, brave and even proud of myself. But, eventually, something even more meaningful happened. By giving myself permission to be authentic, I gave my team permission to do the same.

It started small: team members began sharing more openly in meetings, even when their ideas weren't fully fleshed out. I remember one colleague, who had always been hesitant to speak up, suddenly saying, 'This might sound crazy, but what if we tried . . .' It was an idea that sparked a fantastic discussion and ultimately led to one of our most successful campaigns. Another team member confided in me about struggling with a project timeline, something they would've previously kept quiet about, afraid it might reflect badly on them. Instead of hiding it, we worked together to adjust the plan, and the project ended up running smoother than expected.

I also noticed how the energy in the room changed during our meetings. People were challenging each other's ideas, laughing more and building on one another's thoughts. Conversations became more honest and creativity flourished. Trust grew because we weren't wasting energy on pretending to be something we weren't. We were real with each other, and *that made all the difference*.

This learning curve taught me something fundamental: we must stop trying to be perfect, and instead start trying to be real. And when you're real, you create an environment where others feel safe to be real too.

Along the way in my Boss Era journey, I discovered a handful of practical exercises that helped me shed the need to perform and allowed me to lead with confidence. These tools became the foundation of how I show up. In the next section, we'll explore these exercises so you can begin your own journey towards authentic leadership. Let's dive in.

Five Tools to Become a More Authentic Version of Yourself

I know that breaking free from ingrained habits in a push to become more authentic feels daunting, but it's one of the most liberating and transformative things you'll ever do for yourself – and for those around you. When you let go of the need to please everyone, you create space for yourself to connect more deeply and thus become the best leader you can be.

Authenticity means showing up as your whole self, flaws and all. It takes courage and vulnerability, but those qualities build trust. When you stop fearing judgement or failure, you lead with confidence, purpose and resilience.

The journey will feel uncomfortable at times, but it's worth it. These five tools will help you shed inauthenticity and step into the powerful, unstoppable version of yourself. Not invincible, but free from self-doubt and able to move forward with clarity, even in uncertainty.

1. DISCOVER AND COMMUNICATE YOUR STRENGTHS AND WEAKNESSES

Your strengths aren't just the things you're good at – they are the things that strengthen you. They're the activities that leave you feeling energised, fulfilled and motivated. Weaknesses, on the other hand, are the things that drain you, even if you're capable of doing them.

Start by tracking your energy levels for two weeks. At the end of each day, jot down what gave you energy and what left you feeling depleted. For example, you might feel drained after spending hours on spreadsheets or troubleshooting IT issues – not because you're bad at them, but because they don't excite or fulfil you. On the flip side, energising activities might include brainstorming ideas, mentoring team members or presenting to a group. Pay attention to how you feel after each task. Do you feel inspired, excited or like you could keep going? Or do you feel deflated, frustrated or just relieved to have it over with?

Once you've identified these patterns, share them with your team. Be honest about where you excel and where you need support. For me, I realised that operational admin work completely zapped my energy – it left me feeling stuck and uninspired. But strategy sessions and creative problem-solving? Those made me feel alive. By acknowledging this, I was able to delegate more of the draining tasks and double down on the work that energised me, which ultimately made me a better manager. We will dive deep into leaning into your strengths (and not focusing on your weaknesses) in the next chapter, because when you lead from your strengths, you not only show up better, you also set an example for your team, empowering them to do the same.

2. PEEL BACK THE LAYERS

Underlying fears and anxieties often shape our behaviours. These can include fears of rejection, judgement, failure or even not living up to expectations. Recognising these fears and how they influence your reactions is key to becoming more self-aware and authentic in your leadership.

Think about the last time you felt uneasy or frustrated at work. Was it during a tense meeting, when your ideas weren't acknowledged or when you received unexpected feedback?

Ask yourself why that situation triggered you, and then start peeling back the layers. For example, if you felt dismissed in a meeting, was the real issue a fear of not being taken seriously or perhaps a belief that your ideas needed to be perfect to have value? Digging deeper helps uncover the root of your reaction.

For me, I remember a time early in my management career when I avoided giving a team member constructive feedback. I told myself it was to 'keep the peace', but the truth was deeper than that. When I peeled back the layers, I realised I was scared they might think I was being unfair or that I wasn't experienced enough to offer valid criticism. That fear of being judged held me back from having an honest conversation – and it didn't serve either of us.

Next time you're triggered, take a moment to reflect. Write down:

- The situation that triggered you.

- Your immediate reaction (for example, frustration, avoidance or over-explaining).

- The 'why' behind your reaction: what fear or anxiety might be driving it?

Over time, patterns will emerge that can guide your growth. For example, you might notice that a fear of failure triggers perfectionist behaviours or that a fear of judgement makes you hesitate to share ideas. Naming these triggers gives you the power to address them.

Sheryl Sandberg, former COO of Facebook, shared in her book *Lean In* how she initially hesitated to speak up in meetings because of her fear of being wrong. By examining this fear, she realised it stemmed from perfectionism. Once she identified the trigger, she reframed her mindset, learning to embrace vulnerability and speak up anyway.

3. TELL YOUR STORIES

Stories are one of the most powerful tools a leader has to build trust and inspire. Sharing your own struggles and lessons learned creates a culture of openness and growth.

One time while I was working at Sage, one of my teams was working on a pretty fast-moving project with a tight deadline. One of the team members made a significant mistake that delayed the timeline by days. My instinct was to fix it quietly and move on, but instead, I chose to share my own story. I told them about a mistake I'd made recently – how I'd miscalculated a budget that led to us losing a potential client. I shared how embarrassed I'd felt at the time, but also how I'd learned to own my mistakes, focus on solutions and grow from the experience.

When I opened up about my own misstep, I saw an immediate shift. The team member stopped panicking and instead became more focused on fixing the issue. It also opened the door for others to share their challenges in future projects. That moment reminded me how vulnerability breeds trust and how storytelling can turn a mistake into an opportunity for growth.

Satya Nadella, CEO of Microsoft, who we met in Rule #1, transformed the company's culture by doing something similar – sharing his own experiences with vulnerability. He frequently talks about how his journey as the parent of a child with special needs shaped his empathy and leadership style, encouraging his team to embrace empathy and resilience.

Identify a personal story that illustrates a key leadership

principle you value. Share it at your next team meeting to invite others to do the same. When leaders tell their stories, we show that it's okay to be human.

4. DEFINE YOUR OWN VALUES

Authenticity starts with knowing what you truly stand for. Your values are the guiding principles that influence how you think, act and lead. But identifying them can feel abstract. Think about activities or decisions that consistently bring you energy and satisfaction. What common threads run through these experiences? Use these questions to help:

- When do I feel most like myself?

- What traits do I admire in others?

- What would I fight for, even in difficult circumstances?

Using your reflections, list five to ten values that resonate with you. Examples might include:

- growth

- curiosity

- integrity

- boldness

- community

- empathy

- achievement

5. DROP THE FAÇADE (BIT BY BIT)

Authenticity shines in the little moments. Admitting when you don't know the answer, using clear and conversational language, and showing your human side creates trust and respect. Choose one small way to be more real this week. It could be as simple as replacing a jargon-filled email with straightforward language, openly admitting a mistake or sharing a personal insight during a team meeting. These small, intentional steps pave the way for deeper connections, stronger trust and a more open and collaborative culture.

Step into Your Authenticity

When I think back to the 21-year-old Heather on the shop floor at Harrods, I almost want to reach through time and gently shake her. I'd tell her that the very things she was working so hard to hide – her accent, her quirky ideas, her unpolished leadership style – were her superpowers, not her weaknesses. But, of course, she had to learn that for herself. And so will you.

In those early days, I thought leadership meant smoothing out my edges, hiding my flaws and fitting into the pristine mould of what I believed a 'proper leader' looked like. But here's what I learned: authenticity will not only make you feel more personally powerful, it is also a gift to everyone around you. When you show up as your whole, unapologetic self, you invite others to do the same.

Over time, I've seen the ripple effect authenticity can have. The more I leaned into who I really was, the more my team followed suit. Meetings became less formal and more dynamic. People spoke up more. Ideas flowed freely. Trust started to show in how we communicated. Team members felt safe enough to share both the good and the bad, whether it was celebrating wins or admitting mistakes. I noticed they were more open to giving and receiving feedback because they knew it came from a place of mutual respect, not criticism. Instead of defensiveness, we had honest conversations about what could be improved.

Think about your own journey. What parts of yourself have you hidden because you feared they wouldn't fit the mould? What quirks, strengths or stories are you holding back? What might happen if you stopped trying to fit in and started standing out?

The truth is, no one becomes a remarkable leader by blending in. The leaders we admire – people like Ursula Burns and Satya Nadella – didn't achieve greatness by conforming. They leaned into their individuality, shared their whole selves at work, embraced their vulnerabilities and built cultures where others could thrive by doing the same.

You don't need to wait for permission to be authentic – you already have it. Start small. Share a story. Admit you don't have all the answers. Take off the mask bit by bit. When you do, you'll discover that authenticity is the most powerful leadership tool you have. It builds trust, fuels creativity and inspires the kind of loyalty that can't be bought or forced.

I've been on this journey for years now, and I can tell you this with certainty: it's not always easy, but it's always worth it.

I'll leave you with this thought: the greatest impact you'll ever have as a leader won't come from being right; it will come from being real. So, who are you when the mask comes off?

Lean into that. The world needs it. Your team needs it. And so do you.

And embracing who you truly are isn't *just* about authenticity – it's about leveraging your strengths. Great leaders don't waste time trying to be good at everything; they focus on what they do best.

Don't Improve Your Weaknesses, Play to Your Strengths

I 've worked with countless senior leadership teams, from huge corporates to small, fast-growing businesses, and I see time and time again one clear distinction between middle managers who plateau and those who fly through the ranks to become truly impactful leaders.

The funny thing is, what gets you to climb the ladder in your early career – the ability to take on a variety of tasks, fix problems and progressively improve in all areas of the job – will hold you back from advancing further into your leadership role. Early in our career, we're rewarded for being versatile and dependable, for improving our skill set and tackling our weak points head-on. Think about it: even in interviews, we're primed to answer the classic question, 'What is your greatest weakness?' with an immediate plan to tackle it. It's baked into how we're evaluated and how we perceive our value . . . improving our weaknesses.

But as you climb higher and step into leadership roles, the rules completely change. Leaders at the top aren't successful because they're well-rounded or great at everything – they succeed because they know where they excel and focus their energy there. Great management is about driving results, inspiring teams and creating impact. And you can't do that effectively if you're spreading yourself too thin or pouring energy into areas where you're just not at your best.

When you lean into your strengths, you create the greatest value for your team and organisation. Research by Gallup has shown that when we focus on our strengths, we experience increased confidence, self-awareness and productivity. This strengths-based approach leads to higher employee engagement, improved performance and significantly lower attrition rates. Gallup's studies indicate that teams that focus on strengths every day have 12.5 per cent greater productivity. And workers who learn to use their strengths are 7.8 per cent more productive and have 14.9 per cent lower turnover.

Imagine the difference between a leader who spends hours improving their Excel skills versus one who uses that time to develop and articulate a bold vision for their team. The former might get better at spreadsheets, but the latter builds momentum, rallies people and drives outcomes.

This is also where your career progression and leadership effectiveness start to diverge. Great leaders focus on what they do best and build teams that complement their weaknesses. They create an environment where everyone can excel because they're modelling how to work smarter, not harder. So, while in your early career you may have been celebrated for getting to grips with all the aspects of the job, the next stage requires a different mindset. It's about specialising, doubling down on what strengthens you and surrounding yourself with people who can fill the gaps. Leaders aren't supposed to be superheroes – they're meant to harness the superpowers of their team.

In this chapter, we'll explore how to identify your strengths, lean into them fully and use them to elevate not just your career, but also your ability to lead and inspire others.

How Do I Find My Strengths?

Contrary to popular belief, a strength is not only something you're good at. A strength is something that *strengthens* you. It's the work you could do all day and still feel energised by at the end of it. There's a key psychological concept here: flow, a term coined by psychologist Mihaly Csikszentmihalyi in 1975 who conducted extensive research on optimal experiences and engagement, which laid the foundation for the concept. Flow is the state where you're so immersed in an activity that time seems to fly, you feel fully engaged and the experience leaves you feeling fulfilled rather than drained. You may have heard terms like 'flow state' or 'deep focus' – well, these all relate to working on things that put us in this state of flow. A strength will naturally do this. It's an activity that feels effortless in the best way – not because it's easy, but because it aligns with your core talents and values.

For me, problem-solving and strategy are my strengths. I thrive in quick, slightly chaotic environments where I can make decisions, solve challenges and keep everything moving forward. But attention to detail? That's not my bag. While I can focus when it's critical, tasks that need meticulous review leave me drained and frustrated. For years, I thought this was a huge shortcoming of mine that I had to fix. I had it in my head that the only way for me to progress was being able to do *everything*. But the more I pushed myself to improve my weaknesses, the more I realised I was just taking time and energy away from the things I'm actually brilliant at. Recognising that difference allowed me to lean into what I do best and delegate or collaborate on the rest.

With this in mind, let's walk through an exercise to identify your greatest strengths.

FIND YOUR STRENGTHS EXERCISE

You'll need about 15 minutes to run through this step-by-step exercise, complete with examples and clear outcomes.

Reflect on peak experiences

- **Think about past wins.** Look back at moments when you felt you were at your absolute best at work or in life. What were you doing? Why did it feel so good? Maybe you delivered a big presentation and felt completely in your element, confident and energised. Or perhaps you took control of a spreadsheet or reorganised a chaotic system into something efficient and clear.

- **Write it down.** List three to five specific situations where you felt effective, proud and in control.

Identify common themes

- **Analyse your stories.** Look for recurring patterns in your experiences. What skills or activities were involved? Were you problem-solving, creating, mentoring or something else? If your wins involved mentoring others or building relationships, a strength might be coaching or collaboration. If you excelled in finding creative solutions, innovation might be a strength.

- **Ask, 'What strengthens me?'** Go a little deeper by asking if these activities leave you feeling energised and motivated or drained and exhausted.

Let's say you've realised that you often excel at coordinating large-scale projects. You're great at juggling timelines, ensuring everyone stays on track and pulling together the final deliverables. But does it *strengthen* you?

If you feel energised and motivated every time you create a plan or facilitate teamwork, project management might be one of your strengths. You find joy in organising chaos and guiding a team towards a shared goal. However, if you excel at these tasks but feel drained or frustrated afterwards – if you think, *I can do this, but I really don't enjoy it* – then project management may simply be a skill you've mastered, not a true strength. In that case, look for the underlying activity that does energise you. Perhaps it's the creative brainstorming sessions at the start of the project or the coaching you provide to individual team members. Those might be your real strengths, and they deserve more of your focus.

This exercise should differentiate between what you're *good at* and what genuinely gives you energy, allowing you to focus on work that lights you up and leaves you feeling fulfilled.

Seek feedback from others

- **Ask for outside perspectives.** Reach out to trusted colleagues, friends or family members. Ask them:

  ○ 'When have you seen me at my best?'

  ○ 'What do you think my greatest strength is?'

  ○ 'What do you think I do better than most people?'

- **Compare feedback to your reflections.** Look for overlap between what they see and what you've experienced.

Create your strengths list

- **Summarise your findings.** Write down three to five strengths that stand out from your reflections, feedback and assessments. Your list might look like this for example:

  1. Strategic thinking: I excel at seeing the big picture and mapping out a clear path forward.

  2. Relationship building: I naturally create strong connections with others, which builds trust and collaboration.

  3. Problem-solving: I thrive in situations where I can troubleshoot and find solutions under pressure.

  4. Creativity: I come up with fresh, innovative ideas to tackle challenges.

  5. Communication: I convey complex ideas in a way that's clear and engaging.

By the end of this exercise, you should have a solid list of strengths you can really lean into at work. These are the tasks that genuinely energise you, the ones that leave you feeling stronger and more fulfilled at the end of the day. Use this list as your guide. Focus on work that plays to your strengths and look for ways to develop them further.

When you operate in this space, you're far more likely to experience that magical state of *flow* – when everything just clicks. It's where your natural abilities meet meaningful challenges, and it's a game changer for how you work.

One of the most striking examples of leaning into strengths comes from a former colleague of mine, a senior sales leader named Alejandro. Alejandro had an incredible ability to think on his feet and connect with people. He absolutely thrived in client-facing roles, effortlessly building trust and leaving clients feeling heard and valued, as well as communicating the sales vision for his team. But when it came to managing timelines or overseeing the operational details of a project, it was a completely different story. He could do it when absolutely necessary, but the stress of tracking every moving piece left him drained and frustrated, pulling his focus away from what he did best.

The turning point for Alejandro came when he realised that trying to manage every detail wasn't just exhausting him – it was holding the team back. He eventually brought in a project manager who was incredible with organisation and structure, someone who lived for timelines and operational flow. By doing this, Alejandro was able to lean fully into his strengths, focusing on building relationships, pitching new ideas and driving client success.

What made Alejandro a great leader was his self-awareness. By acknowledging where he added the most value and delegating the rest, he set an example for his team. They followed his lead, openly sharing their own strengths and weaknesses.

This is the power of leaning into your strengths as a leader. It's not just about making your own work feel more fulfilling – it's about setting the tone for your team too. When you model what it looks like to play to your strengths and delegate the rest, you create space for everyone else to do the same.

Recognising your strengths is about freeing yourself to do work that energises and fulfils you. It's about staying in flow as much as possible. But we also need to talk about the other side of the coin: our weaknesses. Knowing what they are, and what to do about them, is just as vital.

Leaning into your strengths doesn't mean avoiding your weaknesses altogether. It means being intentional about where you focus your energy, and finding strategies to handle the rest in a way that works for you and your team.

How Do I Find My Weaknesses?

It's a widely held belief that working on our weaknesses is the key to personal growth. But psychology suggests otherwise. The Pareto Principle, or the 80/20 rule, tells us that 80 per cent of our results often come from just 20 per cent of our efforts. When we focus on our strengths – the areas where we naturally excel – we maximise that 20 per cent. On the flip side, pouring energy into improving our weaknesses can result in diminishing returns. In other words, trying to fix everything you're not good at pulls time and energy away from the things that create real impact. The more you focus on your weaknesses, the less space you have to fully develop and leverage your strengths.

The key isn't to try and muscle through these weaknesses – it's to work smarter by finding ways to manage or delegate them. That's how you create the bandwidth in your energy to focus on what you're brilliant at and truly move the needle. So, now you've pinpointed your strengths, it's time to face the other side of the coin. We need to stop seeing our weaknesses as failures, but instead as simply tasks or skills that don't align with how we're wired.

As I've mentioned, one of the biggest challenges for me has always been attention to detail. I remember the first time I hired someone who genuinely loved the small details I dreaded. Whether it was double-checking reports, managing spreadsheets or refining processes, they absolutely thrived on precision and getting their work spot on. Tasks that would have driven me up the wall, and would have likely not been done in an exacting manner had I taken them on, they actually *enjoyed*.

The first time I handed over those responsibilities felt like a weight had been lifted. I could finally focus on the things I was great at: building strategy, solving big-picture problems and energising my team. It transformed the way we worked as a team and how well I could operate as a leader.

FIND YOUR WEAKNESSES EXERCISE

So, how do you identify your weaknesses? Run through the questions below – again, it'll take about 15 minutes.

Reflect on tasks that drain you

- Think about your daily work. What tasks leave you feeling frustrated, bored or mentally exhausted? For me, it's anything requiring meticulous attention to detail, like proofreading long documents or creating detailed spreadsheets.

Look for patterns

- Are there certain types of work you consistently avoid, procrastinate on or find yourself dreading? These are often areas where you lack energy or natural ability.

- If you consistently avoid tackling administrative tasks, organisation might not be your strength.

Ask for feedback

- Talk to your team, colleagues or manager and ask:

  ○ 'What do you think I could improve on?'

  ○ 'Where do you think I struggle the most?'

Refine your answers

- Write down two to three tasks or activities that consistently drain you and that your colleagues have also highlighted as areas of potential improvement. These are likely to be areas of weakness.

- Then, ask yourself:

  ○ Can I delegate these tasks to someone who does them better than me?

  ○ Is there a tool or system that could help me manage them better?

  ○ Are these tasks even necessary, or can they be deprioritised or eliminated altogether?

Recognising your weaknesses means giving yourself permission to focus on what you do best. It's freeing, but it's also practical.

While delegating the tasks you don't enjoy or aren't naturally good at to others who excel in those areas is ideal, it's not always possible. Sometimes, the job simply has to get done, and it's on you to do it. When that's the case, there are still ways to manage the work that doesn't excite or energise you without it becoming overwhelming. It's about finding ways to approach those tasks with purpose and efficiency. Instead of dreading them, look for ways to minimise their impact on your energy. Could you batch similar tasks together to reduce context switching? Could you schedule them for a time of day when your focus is naturally higher?

As you now know, detailed work has never been my favourite, but I've learned to handle it by creating systems and boundaries. I batch tasks that require intense focus, like reviewing reports or prepping for a big presentation, so I'm not switching between energy-draining work and tasks I enjoy. I also schedule those tasks during times when I know my concentration is at its peak (usually first thing in the morning).

And here's the key: even when you have to tackle work that doesn't energise you, understanding your strengths can still help. If you're a natural problem-solver, approach those tasks like a puzzle to solve. If you thrive on collaboration, involve someone who might enjoy the work more or can provide insight.

The important thing is balance. By focusing most of your energy on the work that strengthens you and finding efficient ways to manage the rest, you create space for yourself and your team to thrive.

This Same Principle Applies to Your Team

Everyone on your team has strengths that energise them and weaknesses that drain them. As a manager, one of the most impactful things you can do is help each person lean into what they're great at and let go of the things they're not, while ensuring the job still gets done.

As part of Gallup's extensive research on employee engagement and performance, they analysed data from approximately 2.7 million employees across 276 companies in 54 industries and 96 countries, and found that employees who use their strengths daily are *six times* more likely to be engaged at work and *three times* more likely to report having an excellent quality of life. These findings really show how important it is to focus on people's strengths.

Here's a small tip that's worked wonders for me: ask each team member, 'If I could take one thing off your plate that would relieve you of the most stress and worry, what would it be?' The answers are always enlightening. Nine times out of ten, the tasks that stress people out the most are the ones that don't play to their strengths. When you take those tasks off their plate and reassign them to someone who thrives on them, it's an opportunity to massively empower your team.

I saw this with Sam, a creative powerhouse on my team who struggled with details, and Claire, who thrived on structure but hesitated to share ideas. After a chaotic campaign, I switched things up: Sam focused on brainstorming and content, while Claire owned the project management.

The result? Campaigns ran smoother, deadlines were met and both of them felt more confident and engaged. By leaning into their strengths, the team thrived – and so did the work.

Or, sometimes, you even realise that task isn't as critical as you thought. I've learned that some things can just be thrown out altogether. You'll often hear me say, 'Let's leave this and revisit it in three months if it's still important.' More often than not, it isn't.

Getting your team working to their strengths is a leadership strategy that transforms productivity, morale and overall success. By helping each person do what they do best, you're creating a team that's energised and resilient.

The Art of Focus

The ability to focus on what truly matters is a skill that separates good managers from great leaders. I have directly trained hundreds of middle managers across the globe, and one of their greatest pitfalls is the temptation to try to fix everything, to be the go-to person for every issue, every challenge and every small problem – to jump in and be the saviour and the rescuer. But, as you step into senior leadership, your role changes; leaders must get much more deliberate and intentional with their time and energy.

The reason this shift is essential is grounded in 'decision fatigue', a psychological concept coined by psychologist Roy Baumeister, that highlights how our capacity to make good decisions diminishes as we're forced to make more of them. Every decision, no matter how small, drains cognitive energy. By spreading ourselves too thin, trying to be everything to everyone, we exhaust ourselves and make poorer choices in the areas that really matter.

Learning to focus was a game changer for me. Early in my leadership journey, I felt like I had to be involved in everything. If there was a problem, I was there to solve it. If something needed improving, I wanted my fingerprints on it. But it very quickly became unsustainable.

I remember one particular week when I'd overcommitted myself completely. I had a to-do list the length of my arm of approvals and answers I needed to get to my team, all while preparing for a major strategy meeting with the directors at our company. By the end of the week, I was completely drained, and I hadn't brought my best to *any* of those tasks. Worse, my team was left waiting for me to make decisions they could have handled better without me.

I knew I needed to step back and reassess how I was spending my time. I started by asking myself three key questions before jumping into any task or project:

1. Does this align with my strengths?

2. Will my involvement make a meaningful impact?

3. Is this something someone else on my team is better equipped to handle?

Answering these questions started shifting things. Instead of being the bottleneck for every decision, I focused on the tasks and decisions that truly moved the needle. And by letting go of the rest, I empowered my team to take ownership of areas where they excelled.

Focusing on less doesn't mean doing less,
it means doing better.

When you narrow your focus to the tasks that only you can do, you conserve your cognitive energy for the most important decisions. You avoid spreading yourself so thin that nothing gets your full attention.

And the best part is, when you focus on what matters, you're not just making yourself more effective, you're setting the tone for your team to do the same. You're showing them how to prioritise, how to let go of tasks that don't align with their strengths and how to concentrate on the areas where they can make the biggest difference.

The myth that great leaders are flawless or well-rounded couldn't be further from the truth. Great leaders are human. They have strengths, weaknesses and, most importantly, the wisdom to know the difference.

And when you embrace your strengths, you're setting a powerful example for your team too. You're showing them that it's okay to lean into what energises them, to let go of what drains them and to ask for support when they need it. You're giving people permission to bring their best selves to the table, to work in ways that fulfil them and to contribute in ways that only they can.

So, as you close this chapter, take a moment to think about where you're focusing your energy. Are you spending it on the work that truly moves the needle, both for you and for your team? Are you leaning into your strengths and giving others the space to lean into theirs?

If not, start today. Choose to let go of the things that don't serve you, delegate with intention and focus on the areas where you can create real impact. Leadership is a journey of constant growth and change, and this is your invitation to take the next step forward.

We've explored the people skills and the human side of leadership – the heart of what makes a great leader – but even the strongest soft skills fall apart without the foundation of unshakeable processes and systems. In the next part, we'll dive into the hard skills you need to build and sustain that foundation, ensuring you and your team can excel in the long run.

Part 2

Systems: Mastering the Mechanics

Systems create clarity and structure so your team knows where they stand. They create repeatable processes that allow your team to thrive. In this part, I'm giving you the tried-and-tested processes I've used over the past decade to help leaders transform their teams and businesses. These proven leadership systems are the frameworks and processes that sit behind some of the most successful teams I've worked with – from global corporations in music and tech to local accountancy firms.

Why Do We Need Systems?

I know you've probably been told over and over that you need to 'systemise', but what does it mean? And why are systems important? The best teams don't run on guesswork. They run on systems. Not rigid rules or bureaucracy, but clear, repeatable processes that keep everyone moving in the same direction without constantly needing to stop and figure things out.

When you have repeatable systems in place – whether it's for setting priorities, giving feedback or making decisions – you free up mental energy that would otherwise be wasted on figuring out what to do next. Your team isn't stuck guessing. They know the process, they trust it, and that consistency gives them the freedom to think bigger, solve problems and focus on doing their best work.

At first, the idea of more systems might sound like it's going to box people in. But the opposite is true. Think about it: if your team is constantly wondering, 'What's the next step?' or 'How do we make this decision?', they're burning through energy on unnecessary thinking. That leads to decision fatigue and slows everyone down.

But when you've got a clear system in place – from your 1-on-1 system to your KPI-hitting system – you take that guesswork out of the equation. People know how things work. They know what's expected. And that clarity creates freedom for creativity, innovation and problem-solving.

It's like running a relay race. If every runner knows exactly when and where to pass the baton, the team runs smoothly. But if no one's sure about the handover points, the whole thing falls apart. And, what's repeatable can be improved.

When you systemise how you run meetings, set goals or give feedback, you create a baseline. And once you have that baseline, you can refine it. You can spot what's working, tweak what's not and make small changes that have a big impact over time.

There's a misconception that systemisation is about control – that putting processes in place will make things rigid and stifle creativity. But that's not true. Systemisation is about clarity. It's about creating enough structure so that people feel safe and empowered to do their best work, without micromanagement. It's about removing the friction that gets in the way of your team's success. Think of it like the guardrails on a motorway. You're not telling people exactly how to drive – you're just making sure they stay on the right track and don't crash.

Finally, systems free you up as a leader. When you're not constantly answering the same questions or making every decision yourself, you have time to focus on the big-picture stuff. The vision. The strategy. The people. And that's where true leadership happens.

When your team trusts the systems, they can operate independently. They feel empowered to make decisions within the framework you've set. And that's when you, as a leader, can finally begin to step out of the day-to-day firefighting and focus on driving long-term success.

The systems I'm sharing in this section are blueprints that I've tested, tweaked and perfected after countless rounds of trying, failing and going again.

And now? They're yours.

Ready to dive in? Let's go.

Get to Know Your Team (the 1-on-1 System)

As a new manager, I was always proud of my 'open-door' policy. I figured if my team needed something, they'd come to me. After all, I was friendly, available and willing to help whenever they asked, right? But that approach didn't exactly create the results I expected. Instead of building the trust and free communication that I'd hoped for, I noticed silences in meetings, hesitations around feedback and a lack of any proactive problem-solving.

It didn't take long for frustration to creep in around said proud open-door policy. I couldn't understand why my team wasn't coming to me with issues or ideas. I had made it clear that I was there for them, so why did it feel like I was always the last to know when something went wrong? Why weren't they stepping up to solve problems or share solutions?

So one day, I just straight up asked a team member. Their response stopped me in my tracks: 'I didn't want to bother you. I know you're busy.' That was when it hit me – my 'open-door' policy wasn't the safety net I thought it was. It put all the responsibility on *them* to decide when and how to approach me. In their eyes, I was approachable, but inconsistent. There was no structure, no expectation and no space carved out for the conversations that really mattered.

Over the following few months, I started to backtrack. I needed a reliable, consistent system for 1-on-1 check-ins with the team, so I wasn't relying on them to bring issues to me. I started by scheduling weekly meetings with each team member – short, focused and non-negotiable, attempting to create a regular rhythm of trust and communication.

The result? Problems started getting raised earlier (and often came with potential solutions already attached). And the final evidence I needed was when my team survey results came back. The scores showed they were more engaged, and they felt as though their voices were heard. I no longer needed to worry what was going on in their world, or pre-empt problems, because we had a space to share it.

Trust and communication can't be built through vague policies like an 'open door'. They require a system, coupled with consistent action. A 1-on-1 system should be viewed as the foundation for your team to thrive on, not as random 'check-in' meetings or yearly appraisals.

Over the years, I tested and refined my system relentlessly. I experimented with different meeting frequencies – weekly, fortnightly, monthly – to see what worked best in various team dynamics. I tried asking open-ended questions, struc-tured prompts and even rapid-fire check-ins. Each iteration taught me something new about what teams need and how us managers can create a space where people feel safe, heard and empowered.

Eventually, I landed on a tried-and-tested 1-on-1 system that has become the backbone of how I lead – and, more importantly, since I have shared this system online, it is now how thousands of managers lead their teams across the globe. It's the only 1-on-1 system every manager needs to implement in their team.

Since its release, it has been downloaded and used by over 10,000 managers globally. I've seen how it transforms team dynamics across industries, from small start-ups to multinational corporations. Teams become more engaged, more proactive and more cohesive. Managers finally step out of their reactive firefighting mode and instead embrace strategic, confident leadership.

The Mistakes

Before we dive into the exact model of the perfect 1-on-1 system, it's important to address some common mistakes I see often.

MISTAKE 1: ASSUMING YOUR TEAM'S PRIORITIES ARE THE SAME AS YOUR OWN

It's easy to think your team shares your ambitions: promotions, pay rises and career progression. But their priorities might be entirely different. Maybe they're more focused on spending time with their kids, achieving work–life balance or pursuing personal projects outside of work. Without understanding what drives them, it's impossible to lead in a way that will inspire them. You could end up pushing them towards goals they don't care about.

I learned this lesson the hard way. Once upon a time, I assumed everyone on my team valued the same things I did. At the time, I was of course younger than I am now, with no partner, no kids and no mortgage. My focus was laser-sharp on climbing the ladder, getting promotions and hitting the next big career milestone. But many of my team members had completely different priorities. Some were parents, balancing work with school runs and bedtime stories. Others were deeply motivated by freedom or creativity, rather than the corporate hustle.

When I assumed they cared about the same things I did, it not only held them back, it also created a sense of disconnect within the team. I'd push them towards goals that didn't excite them or fit with their lives, and it showed. Their engagement wavered, communication became strained and the results we could have achieved as a team fell flat.

Regular 1-on-1 meetings are not only essential, they provide a platform to uncover those individual priorities: personal goals, challenges and aspirations.

By actively listening and tailoring support to align with individual team members' unique motivations, you'll build a much more engaged and productive team. It's a win–win: job satisfaction increases, turnover decreases and, most importantly, your team feels valued and understood. This connects back to the intrinsic motivators we explored in Rule #3 – when people feel a sense of purpose, autonomy, and mastery in their work, their engagement and performance naturally rise. By recognising and aligning with what drives them, you're not just improving job satisfaction; you're tapping into the deeper forces that sustain long-term motivation and success.

Looking back, I wish I'd realised sooner that being a manager should never end up with us expecting everyone to fit into our version of success. Instead, we should focus on creating environments where each person can thrive in their own way. Regular 1-on-1s are how you make that happen.

MISTAKE 2: ONLY DOING 'APPRAISALS' ONCE A YEAR

Relying solely on annual appraisals is like trying to fix a leaky roof after a year of storms – it's far too late. An annual appraisal bottles up feedback, praise and opportunities for growth until one big meeting, which just doesn't work. It creates unnecessary pressure and misses the chance to address issues or celebrate wins when they're still relevant.

I learned this lesson not just as a manager, but as an employee on the other side of the table too. Early in my career, I worked under a manager who didn't provide much feedback (if any), good or bad. The promise of an annual appraisal was dangled as the only opportunity to discuss my performance, progression or development. The problem was, I wasn't willing to wait an entire year to find out where I stood or to address the mounting frustrations I felt about my role.

I remember feeling increasingly disconnected from my work, not knowing if I was doing well or missing the mark – anxious on a Sunday, fearful about making even the smallest of mistakes. Then one day, after a particularly tense week, I'd hit my limit. I handed in my notice before the appraisal even rolled around. I never even heard what my manager thought of my performance because, frankly, it was too little, too late.

This experience stuck with me when I moved into management. I realised how damaging it can be to rely on a once-a-year feedback system. It leaves our team in the dark, and puts us at risk of losing great employees who feel undervalued or unsure of their future.

Regular 1-on-1 meetings are the antidote to the shortcomings of annual appraisals. These consistent check-ins create ongoing opportunities to discuss progress, address concerns and celebrate achievements in real time. According to a Gallup study, employees who receive weekly feedback are 3.6 times more likely to be engaged at work.

By building a rhythm of open communication, you take the guesswork out of performance management – no more surprises at the end of the year, no more bottling up feedback. Instead, you create an environment where your team feels supported, seen and valued. That's how you keep great people from walking out the door – and how you drive the kind of growth that benefits everyone.

MISTAKE 3: RELYING ON 'MY DOOR IS ALWAYS OPEN'

Relying on a 'my door is always open' policy is a common mistake. It's just not enough. Even with the best intentions, most team members won't take you up on it. As I learned with my team, they don't want to 'bother' you, especially if they think you're busy or stressed. Without a clear structure in place, the door may be open, but the conversations you're hoping for will rarely, if ever, happen.

Our team needs structure. Because without regular, intentional touchpoints, you're not creating the conditions for meaningful dialogue – you're leaving it in your team's hands.

Our team members are often reluctant to tell us when there's a problem because speaking up feels risky. One major reason for this is a psychological phenomenon called the 'authority gradient', which is the natural power imbalance between leaders and their teams. This natural dynamic creates hesitation, as employees may feel intimidated by your position or worry about how raising an issue will reflect on them. Fear of negative consequences plays a big role; people are more motivated to avoid losses, like damaging their reputation or job security, than to pursue potential gains, such as solving the problem. Even in supportive workplaces, they might think that bringing up a concern will make them seem incompetent, overly critical or a 'troublemaker'.

To overcome this, we have to create an environment which feels safe and where it is encouraged to share challenges, and regular 1-on-1 meetings are key to achieving this. These structured, predictable conversations lower the stakes for employees, providing a dedicated space to discuss concerns without fear of judgement. Over time, this consistency builds trust and erodes the authority gradient, showing your team that their input is valued and acted upon. By implementing this system, you ensure problems are brought to light and tackled early, creating a healthier and more productive team dynamic.

A structured 1-on-1 system does what an open door never could: it proactively invites conversation and strengthens the connection between you and your team.

It's time to stop leaving the door ajar, and instead open it wide at the same predictable time and say, 'This is your time. Let's talk.'

The Method

Now, let's get into the practical solution – the 1-on-1 system I've developed over years of trial, error and fine-tuning.

This system is built around four key components that work together to create a rhythm of trust, accountability and alignment in your team. And you can take it away and implement it today.

THE ROBUST 1-ON-1 SYSTEM

Here's the overview of each meeting you should be doing with every one of your direct reports:

- **Every day**: Regular, unmissed moments of praise and, when necessary, direct but caring feedback.

- **Every 2 weeks**: A 30-minute, no-agenda check-in to create space for open conversations.

- **Every 90 days**: An in-depth 1-on-1 to discuss performance, personal development and alignment. Agenda incoming.

- **Every year**: A salary review (or every six months in smaller, fast-growing companies, where responsibilities are constantly evolving).

Scan the QR code below to download my full 1-on-1 system for you to use with your team:

Before we break down each part, let me explain how these components came together.

STEP 1: PRAISE AND DIFFICULT CONVERSATIONS EVERY DAY

This is where it all begins. Whether it's recognising someone's brilliant work or addressing a problem, it's something we need to commit to every day – it's the very foundation of building a strong team. Not just in formal settings, but in real time, as it happens. It keeps things moving, shows your team you're paying attention and stops little issues from becoming big ones.

I learned this the hard way early on. One of my first team members was consistently missing deadlines, and I kept putting off saying anything. They were new to the job and I didn't want to come across as overly critical – especially since I worried I'd start sounding picky about everything. *Give them time to find their feet*, I kept telling myself, even as the delays piled up. But, deep down, I knew I was avoiding the conversation because I didn't want to make them feel demoralised or unsupported.

Eventually, though, the problem became impossible to ignore. The rest of the team was feeling the knock-on effects, and I realised that staying silent wasn't kind – it was unfair. So, I decided to address it. Before sitting down with them, I spent time thinking about how to approach the conversation.

When we finally spoke, I explained how the missed deadlines were impacting the team and asked if they were okay or if something was getting in the way of their work. To my surprise, they weren't defensive at all. They admitted they'd been feeling overwhelmed by the workload and were afraid to ask for help because they didn't want to seem incapable in a new role. They even suggested a few changes – small adjustments to deadlines and priorities – that could help them stay on track without feeling overloaded.

That conversation didn't fix the problem immediately, but it completely changed the way I thought about feedback. Feedback is a gift – the kind of gift that can change the trajectory of someone's career, unlock their potential and strengthen bonds. As we explored in Rule #2, tough feedback, when delivered with care, shows your team you're in their corner. It says, 'I'm invested in helping you grow.' It's one of the greatest acts of leadership you can offer.

So the key here is to make praise and feedback a regular habit, not something you save up for 1-on-1s or performance reviews. When you do, it keeps your team feeling valued and clear on what's working and what needs to change. Ignoring feedback, whether it's positive or constructive, sends its own message: that their efforts don't matter or, worse, that poor performance is fine. Neither is good for anyone.

Don't let things fester. Speak up, taking care you do it in appropriate settings and in private if it's a tough conversation. Your team will thank you for it – and you'll thank your future self for it too.

STEP 2: 30-MINUTE CHECK-INS EVERY 2 WEEKS

If daily praise and feedback are the foundation, then these 30-minute, fortnightly check-ins are the scaffolding that keeps everything standing strong. These sessions give you the chance to go deeper, to explore more nuanced challenges and opportunities that can't always be tackled in the moment. A recurring 30-minute meeting without a rigid agenda might not sound revolutionary, but when done consistently, it absolutely is.

I saw the power of these check-ins first-hand when I introduced them early in my leadership journey. At the time, I was constantly fielding questions and concerns from my team throughout the day. It felt like I was putting out fires, one Slack message at a time, and I knew something had to change. But I knew weekly 1-on-1s would take up too much of my time, so I committed to fortnightly check-ins with each team member.

At first, the sessions felt a little awkward. Some team members didn't know what to bring to the table, and I wasn't entirely sure how to guide the conversation. But I stuck with it and, over time, I watched something powerful happen. Team members began saving their bigger questions and challenges for our check-ins rather than peppering me with messages throughout the day. This not only freed up my time, but also encouraged them to think critically and solve smaller problems on their own before coming to me.

Whenever I speak to managers about installing a 1-on-1 system, they say, 'But I don't have the time among my other priorities', but this system will save you time, not cost you it.

These meetings need to be sacred. Cancelling them, even for something you may consider a valid reason, sends a message that their time isn't as important as yours. It can chip away at the trust you're trying to build. Even if there's no pressing issue, keeping the space open shows your team that you value them and their growth.

A consistent 30 minutes every 2 weeks might seem small, but, for me, it was the difference between being a reactive leader and an intentional one. Make it a non-negotiable in your calendar – you won't regret it.

STEP 3: IN-DEPTH 1-ON-1S EVERY 90 DAYS

Let's stick with the house-building metaphor. If daily feedback is the foundation and fortnightly check-ins are the scaffolding, then these quarterly in-depth sessions are the blueprints for what comes next. They're the moments where you step back, look at the bigger picture and ensure the structure you're building is solid, aligned and primed for growth.

These 90-day conversations go beyond the day-to-day or even week-to-week concerns. They're about asking the big questions: performance, development and how individual goals align with the team's vision. Think of them as your opportunity to look ahead, identify opportunities and ensure every member of your team is set up for long-term success.

For me, these sessions have replaced the traditional annual appraisal. There's no endless backward-looking or generic form-filling here – just intentional, meaningful dialogue that shapes what comes next.

One key component of these sessions is a question I always ask: 'Which of our company's core values shine through the most in you, and which do you think you need to work on?' Core values are the heart of your organisation's culture. Many of us think core values are wishy-washy and just words on a wall. Incorporating this one question into your 1-on-1s is how you take the words off the wall and actually make them come to life in your team. They're the behaviours and principles that guide how your team works, communicates and grows together. When we bring these values into the conversation, it shifts the focus beyond the individual and into how they contribute to the wider team and culture. Incorporating values into 1-on-1s is how we align with the company's mission. By asking this question, you're encouraging your team member to reflect on how they embody the organisation's values in their day-to-day work. More importantly, you're giving them a chance to identify areas for growth – and you'll reflect on the same question for yourself, too.

And here's the key: this isn't just about giving feedback – it's about getting it too. These sessions are your chance to hear truthfully how you're doing as a leader, uncover blind spots and gain insight into what your team needs from you to thrive. After all, leadership is a two-way street, and we know the best leaders are always learning.

HOW TO SET UP YOUR QUARTERLY MEETING

- Block out 90 minutes of uninterrupted time.
- Use the agenda found in the QR code on the next page.
- Send the agenda to your team member 48 hours beforehand.
- Both of you should fill it out before the session.
- Follow the agenda, but ask more questions and explore where needed.

With a clear plan and open minds, these sessions can become one of the most powerful tools in your leadership toolkit. Scan the QR code below to get the FULL agenda for this session:

STEP 4: SALARY REVIEWS EVERY YEAR (MINIMUM)

Daily feedback is the foundation, fortnightly check-ins are the scaffolding, quarterly deep dives are the blueprints, and then salary reviews are your finishing touches – the final, important section of the structure you're building as a leader. They bring everything together, ensuring your team feels valued, fairly compensated and motivated to keep contributing to the bigger picture.

But, unlike regular feedback or 1-on-1s, salary reviews tend to be more influenced by company structures, policies and budgets. That's why the first step to handling them well is to get really familiar with how your organisation approaches pay reviews. Do raises follow strict performance metrics? Are they tied to company-wide evaluations or budget cycles? Knowing these details will help you navigate the conversation with confidence.

However, there's more to salary reviews than company policies – they're also a key moment to ensure fairness and equity. Research shows that bias regularly creeps into pay decisions, often disadvantaging women, people of colour or others from marginalised groups. Before the meeting, take a moment to review your decisions through an EDI lens. Are there any patterns or pay gaps in your team that need addressing? Are you evaluating contributions objectively or could subjective impressions be influencing your judgement? Use market benchmarks and clear, data-driven performance criteria to make your decisions as transparent and unbiased as possible.

These meetings are most effective when they're planned and intentional. Share the agenda with your team member 48 hours in advance, giving both of you time to prepare. Encourage them to reflect on their achievements, contributions and any development goals they've met. On your side, come armed with the facts: their performance, market benchmarks for their role and any company constraints you need to consider.

Salary reviews can feel high-stakes, but, when done well, they're an opportunity to strengthen trust, ensure equity and deepen your relationship with your team. Approach them with transparency, preparation and empathy, and they can become a cornerstone of long-term engagement and loyalty.

Get to Know Your Team

Let's be real, being a manager often feels like we're juggling a never-ending plate of tasks, and I know this structure will seem like just one more thing to add. But investing in these regular touchpoints will *save you time* in the long run. It cuts down on constant interruptions, builds trust and creates clarity, so you're not firefighting the same issues over and over again.

The goal here isn't to micromanage your team or cater to every little preference – it's about creating a workplace where people genuinely feel heard, valued and supported. This is about building trust, showing that you care and helping your team grow. A healthy workplace is one where people know where they stand, feel like their contributions matter and trust that they're being supported to grow.

These daily, fortnightly, quarterly and annual touchpoints are the building blocks of something pretty amazing – a team built on clarity and real connection. With these strong foundations, you can focus on creating an environment where people feel valued and genuinely want to show up and do their best. Sure, it's a bit of extra work up front, but it's the kind of effort that pays off in the long run.

Next up, we're talking about the art of having difficult conversations. When you're practising Step 1 and giving regular feedback, you'll already have a foundation in place to tackle those tougher talks without the stress.

Have the Courage to Confront

Remember 'Stop being nice, start being kind' back in Rule #2 – and that there's a fundamental difference between being nice and being kind?

Being nice is about giving others satisfaction to make them feel good and winning approval. And in the world of work, this tends to show up in forms of giving feedback in a light-hearted way so as not to hurt people's feelings too much or not giving that feedback at all.

Being kind isn't a complete U-turn, but it's a different way to approach situations, which will yield an entirely different outcome. Being kind is to give feedback directly. A message needs to be delivered in an effective way in order for it to be properly heard and understood, and therefore help the person on the receiving end to grow as a result.

Difficult conversations are (I'm going to say it with my full chest) the HARDEST skill in leadership. And that's because they require the most courage to have.

We've been told our entire life if 'we don't have anything nice to say, don't say it at all', and we spend most of our earlier years avoiding conflict as much as possible, so why would anything change when we move into our management roles?

> A person's success in life can usually be measured by the number of uncomfortable conversations he or she is willing to have.
>
> Tim Ferriss, *The 4-Hour Workweek*

In the world of work (or otherwise), it's easy to fall into the trap of being 'nice'. We shy away from difficult conversations, telling ourselves it's to avoid hurting someone's feelings or creating conflict. On the surface, this approach might seem harmless, even noble. After all, being liked is part of good leadership, right? But let me tell you about the time I watched 'niceness' backfire in a way that fractured an entire team . . .

A manager I worked with – let's call her Priya – was known for being nice, approachable and always steering clear of anything uncomfortable. When a team member, Laura, consistently missed deadlines, Priya never addressed it. She didn't want to come across as harsh or risk upsetting Laura. Instead, she compensated by quietly redistributing the workload to others, hoping no one would notice.

At first, the team appreciated Priya's pleasant demeanour. But, over time, resentment started to bubble beneath the surface. Team members noticed the disparity in workloads and began to talk. 'Why isn't Laura held accountable?' they wondered. Those whispers grew into gossip, creating cliques within the team. People started avoiding Laura, venting about her instead of addressing the issue directly.

And Priya? Her leadership started to lose credibility. The team felt she wasn't being fair, that she prioritised keeping the peace over addressing real problems. Relationships became surface-level because trust had eroded. After all, if Priya couldn't address Laura's shortcomings, how could the rest of the team trust her to stand up for them?

This is what happens when we prioritise being 'nice' over being honest when we're faced with difficult situations. Gossip takes root, dividing teams and creating toxicity. Surface-level relationships lead to a lack of real connection and collaboration. And, as a leader, you risk tarnishing your reputation as someone who can make tough decisions and guide the team with integrity.

Niceness may feel safe in the moment, but it puts a cap on your leadership potential. It keeps you stuck in a place of short-term comfort, while your team quietly crumbles beneath the weight of unresolved issues.

If you want to build a high-performing team, all pushing towards your business goals, these uncomfortable conversations are inevitable.

IF I COULD GO BACK IN TIME . . .

Let's rewind almost a decade: I'm an assistant manager at Harrods in London with a direct team of eight people. Uncomfortable conversations were my biggest fear. Telling someone about their unacceptable lateness, delivering difficult feedback about the standard of their work or, God forbid, firing someone – all these things kept me up at night and I experienced huge anxiety about them. But fast-forward to today, and I've actually grown to love having them. Why? Because I've seen first-hand how kind they are.

When I address lateness with someone, it strengthens them by holding them accountable and giving them a chance to rise to higher standards. It sends the message, 'I believe you're capable of better, and I care enough to tell you.' I've seen team members go from consistently underperforming to becoming some of the most dependable people in the room, because they knew where they stood and felt supported to improve.

When I give constructive feedback about someone's work, it strengthens our relationship by showing them I'm invested in their growth. It demonstrates that I value their contributions enough to help them get better, rather than brushing things under the carpet. One team member once said to me, 'Thank you for telling me the truth – I never realised how much it was holding me back.' That's the power of honest conversations.

And when I've had to let someone go, as hard as it was, I've often found it brought unexpected strength to the team left behind. One person's negative behaviour can drag down an entire group. When you address it, the team feels relieved, knowing that fairness and accountability are priorities. It shows that everyone's effort matters.

These conversations don't just help individuals grow, they deepen trust. They create an environment where people know I'll always be honest, that they'll get both the feedback they need to improve and the support to act on it. Relationships that could have stayed surface-level evolve into partnerships built on mutual respect.

So yes, I've become addicted to these conversations. Because I've learned that, far from being something to fear, they're one of the kindest and most transformative things you can do as a leader.

> The skill of having an uncomfortable conversation is essential in Leadership, and the way you're going to master them is by actually having them.
>
> Simon Sinek

How to Master Difficult Conversations

Difficult conversations will make or break how sustainable the impact of your leadership will be. They are the moments that will earn you respect and build an empowered team – but why?

Imagine you have a team member, let's call her Rachel, who is highly capable but avoids speaking up in meetings. You notice this and, instead of ignoring it, you decide to have a conversation. You tell Rachel that you've noticed her staying quiet during discussions and ask if there's anything holding her back. During the conversation, she shares that she feels nervous about how her ideas will be received. You listen, validate her concerns and share how much you value her perspective. You work together to create a plan for her to contribute more gradually, like starting with smaller updates or ideas in 1-on-1 settings.

The result? Rachel begins to speak up more, her confidence grows and her ideas start to shape the direction of the team's projects. Other team members notice, feel encouraged to share more themselves and the team as a whole becomes stronger and more collaborative. That one conversation didn't just empower Rachel – it created a ripple effect across the team.

This is the power of difficult conversations. When you address issues like underperformance, behavioural concerns or even hidden potential, you create an environment of trust and accountability. People know you're willing to have honest, constructive discussions, and they feel supported to improve, take risks and grow.

Mastering difficult conversations requires a shift in mindset. Instead of shying away from these moments, embrace them as opportunities for growth – for both you and your team. Here are five key steps to help you navigate these conversations effectively:

STEP 1: START WITH YOU

Reflect on your own response to feedback. How do you handle criticism? Do you become defensive or do you see it as an opportunity to improve? Start by asking your team for feedback on your leadership.

But here's the key: don't just ask for feedback, act on it. For example, if your team points out that you tend to dominate conversations in meetings, make a conscious effort to step back and give others more space to contribute. Share with them what you're working on and check in regularly to see if they've noticed an improvement.

By visibly acting on the feedback and communicating your progress, you build trust and show your team that you're not just paying lip service, you're serious about improving. This transparency makes it much more likely that they'll embrace your feedback when the time comes for you to share it with them.

It's also worth reflecting on your leadership style and considering whether you have played a role in any 'issues' that are showing up in the team. Let's use an example of one of my clients, Annabel. She is a senior manager at a mid-sized tech firm. Annabel was having a hard time with one of her developers, Tom. Tom was consistently missing deadlines and seemed disengaged – what most of us would call a 'difficult' employee. Initially, Annabel was convinced that Tom was a bad fit for the team – that he simply didn't care and he

Difficult conversations aren't easy, but they're the foundation of the trust, growth and resilience that define great leadership.

didn't have the right work ethic or the right skills to deliver what she or the company needed.

I asked Annabel one day if she'd considered if she had:

- clearly communicated expectations

- provided the right resources

- created an environment where feedback is both given and received effectively

And it was such an instant light-bulb moment. Annabel realised that she had never clearly communicated expectations to Tom. He didn't have KPIs, he didn't have working hour guidelines, he didn't even have a job description or a 1-on-1 system. She had just assumed he knew the importance of deadlines and the impact his delays had on the team and on the wider business KPIs, but she had never spelled it out to him.

Over the next few weeks and months, Annabel worked on taking accountability first, clarifying expectations, building a 1-on-1 system and giving Tom clarity on his KPIs – and, over time, Tom's performance improved significantly.

Let's revisit the distinction here between being **nice** and being **kind**.

Being nice often means avoiding conflict, sugar-coating feedback or saying yes to everything just to keep the peace. However, being kind requires courage – and sometimes that courage is in accepting that the problem may have been created by you, and be yours to solve. Kindness is about challenging people when necessary, yourself included – and while it may be uncomfortable, it ultimately benefits the individual and the team.

The lesson here is clear: before addressing an employee's behaviour, consider whether you've done everything in your power to support their success. Reflect on your management style, communication and the environment you've created. Are there gaps that you need to address? Accountability is about eradicating blame, recognising your role in the situation and making necessary adjustments.

Let's say you have truly done everything in your power to build an environment for your team members to flourish in, and their behaviour still isn't right and needs addressing. Time to get into . . .

STEP 2: PRACTISE COURAGE

Having difficult conversations in the spirit of being kind is important, but it is absolutely not easy. It doesn't feel natural and it's so much easier to just ignore the thing.

cour·age / *noun*
The ability to do something that frightens one.

And here I'm asking you to do exactly that – frighten yourself.

These conversations aren't easy. It's easier for me today than ever before, but it still isn't comfortable. But that doesn't matter – I'll still always push through that comfort zone barrier and deliver the feedback as needed. Courage isn't a mythical virtue only strong men have when saving a damsel in distress. It is simply a skill, and skills can be learned – all you need to do is practise it in everyday life until it feels normal.

STEP 3: REMIND YOURSELF OF THE PURPOSE

Before entering a difficult conversation, remind yourself why it's important. The words you're about to say might be exactly what the other person needs to hear. Early in my career, I had a team member, Alex, who was underperforming on a big project. Deadlines were being missed and the quality of their work wasn't up to standard. I avoided addressing it at first, thinking they were just having a rough patch and would figure it out. But, as time went on, their behaviour didn't improve, and the rest of the team started to pick up on it. Resentment began brewing because everyone else was working overtime to compensate.

When I finally had the conversation, Alex told me they had no idea their performance was an issue. They admitted they were struggling with time management, but hadn't wanted to ask for help. By addressing it, we were able to make a plan: breaking down tasks, setting smaller milestones and giving Alex more support. Not only did their performance improve, but our working relationship became stronger because they knew I cared enough to have that tough conversation instead of letting them fail silently.

This is why it's so important to remind yourself of the purpose before stepping into a conversation. You're not being confrontational – you're being honest, supportive and proactive in helping the other person succeed.

STEP 4: ADDRESS ISSUES IN THE MOMENT (*ALMOST ALWAYS*)

Address issues as they arise – don't let them fester. The longer you wait, the harder it becomes to have the conversation and the less impactful it will be. Don't allow your own brain to gaslight you, telling yourself, *Was it really that bad though? Maybe I'm overthinking it.* You're not. Have the conversation right then and there. Also, the person on the receiving end is much more likely to remember the circumstances and understand your reasoning if the conversation is had sooner. However, if you're in a highly emotional state, give yourself time to cool down before addressing the issue.

STEP 5: HAVE A METHOD

Having a method means you don't have to get lost and stumble over your own words. Approach the conversation with honesty and integrity. Start by acknowledging the discomfort, express your feelings, outline the specific actions that have caused concern and explain the consequences if the behaviour continues. This method ensures that the conversation is clear, constructive and, most importantly, kind. (Spoiler: The method is not a sh*t sandwich.)

The method

1. **Lean into the discomfort.** You know when something feels awkward and someone goes, 'Well, this is awkward' and it creates a bit of lightness, and there's usually a bit of laughing? Well, that's because someone has leaned into the tension. Start off by saying something like:

   - 'Please be patient with me as I try to get this out.'

   - 'It's important to me that I have this conversation with you.'

- 'I'm a little afraid that I'll say the wrong thing here, so please bear with me.'

2. **Express your feelings.** Explain how you were made to feel by what they did or are doing. Leaders often get hung up on having to 'prove' why we feel a certain way, but if we're struggling to write up evidence, simply telling someone how they've made you feel can be enough. Feelings are valid too.

   We often hold ourselves back from having these conversations because we're worried the person on the receiving end will argue about their actions. We fear not having a detailed list of proof and being 'caught out' without enough evidence. And while evidence is ideal, your feelings are a valid part of any conversation, and they should be treated with respect. Opening up about how someone's actions made you feel is not a weakness – it's a powerful way to model authenticity, clarity and fairness in your leadership.

3. **Describe their actions.** Describe exactly what actions the person has taken that have caused you or others to feel this way. Be specific and factual. This is another reason why having the conversation in the moment is so important – you're far more likely to forget the accurate details if you leave it too long.

   But what if the behaviour is a recurring issue? Whether it's lateness, missing deadlines or inappropriate jokes, keeping track of repeated actions can help you approach the conversation with clarity and confidence. I recommend creating a simple system to document these instances. This could be as straightforward as keeping a private note on your laptop, and jotting down the date, the action and any relevant details shortly after it happens. For example:

- 15th Jan: Late to team meeting by 20 minutes for the third time this month.

- 20th Jan: Made an inappropriate comment about Sarah during lunch; the room became visibly tense.

Writing down these things ensures you're not relying on memory alone, which can be biased or vague over time. It also allows you to spot patterns, making it easier to identify whether something is a one-off mistake or part of a larger issue that needs addressing.

Keeping track isn't about creating a list of grievances to dump on someone – it's about being prepared to have a productive and constructive conversation. When you can present clear examples, you'll reduce the chance of the person being unable to recall specifics or claiming they didn't realise their behaviour was an issue.

Having this record also keeps the conversation focused on the actions, not your emotions, which can make it easier for both parties to stay objective and solution-focused.

4. **Explain the consequence.** Most managers ignore this step. It can feel like the scariest point to make, but that's because it has the most impact. We need to explain to our team member that, if this behaviour continues, they need to understand what the consequences will be. Will they need to move on to performance management?

Will this escalate to a formal disciplinary process? Could it result in them losing their job?

It's crucial to know these answers beforehand. Take the time to understand your company's policies and processes so you're fully prepared to outline the potential consequences during the conversation. For example, review your organisation's performance management guidelines, disciplinary procedures or HR handbook. This preparation ensures you stay aligned with company policy and prevents you from making vague or unrealistic statements.

Consequences will vary depending on the issue. For minor concerns, like missed deadlines or occasional lateness, the next step might be increased check-ins or setting clear performance expectations. For more serious or repeated issues, such as inappropriate behaviour or poor performance, it might involve a formal warning, moving to performance improvement plans (PIPs) or escalating to HR for further action.

When preparing to set down the consequences, think of this step not as a threat but as clarity. It's about giving your team member a roadmap of what will happen if things don't change. For example:

- 'If you miss another project deadline, we'll need to move to a formal performance management plan to address this.'

- 'This is the second time this behaviour has been flagged. If it happens again, we'll need to involve HR to discuss next steps.'

Being clear about the impact doesn't just help you – it also helps your team member. It removes any ambiguity and leaves them with a full understanding of what's at stake. Without this clarity, there's a high chance the conversation won't be taken seriously, and the behaviour is unlikely to change.

5. **Make sure you follow up.** The conversation doesn't end once it's over. One of the most important steps in handling difficult conversations is the follow-up. This ensures accountability, clarity and a shared understanding of what was discussed and agreed upon.

    Start by documenting the conversation. This doesn't mean you need to write a novel, just a clear summary of the key points. Include:

    • what the issue was

    • the feedback you provided

    • any actions or behaviour changes agreed upon

    • the potential consequences if the issue persists

    • the agreed-upon next steps or check-in date

    This documentation isn't just for your records; it can also be helpful if the issue escalates or if you need to involve HR at a later stage. Once you've documented the conversation, follow up with a recap email to your team member. This step is crucial for ensuring you're both on the same page and eliminates any room for misunderstanding. For example, you might say:

Hi [Name],

I wanted to follow up on our conversation earlier today to make sure we're aligned. We discussed [briefly summarise the issue], and I appreciate your willingness to address it.

As agreed, the next steps are [outline next steps]. I'll check in with you on [date] to review progress and discuss how things are going. Please let me know if you have any questions or need support in the meantime.

This email serves as a written record of the conversation while also showing your commitment to supporting them in making the necessary changes.

Finally, make sure to follow through on your commitments. If you've said you'll check in at a specific time, stick to it. Following up consistently signals that you take these matters seriously and that you're invested in their growth and success. It also reinforces accountability, showing that you expect actions, not just words, in response to the conversation.

The follow-up process isn't micromanaging or adding pressure, it's showing that you truly care about progress, keeping communication open and making sure the issue gets resolved.

Mastering difficult conversations is a journey. It's not something that happens overnight, but with practice and the right mindset, you'll become more comfortable and effective in having these crucial discussions.

But what about when you've had the discussions over and over again, but nothing has changed – what then?

Performance Management

Performance management is a really effective tool that, when done right, can help turn around an employee's performance and set them up to succeed. It's not something that's used for everyone – it's a more structured process designed to tackle performance issues when regular chats and feedback just haven't done the trick. Think of it as the next step when things need a bit more focus and formality.

Performance management provides a clear pathway for addressing performance issues by:

- setting measurable, time-bound expectations for improvement

- providing regular and specific feedback tied to those expectations

- offering structured support, such as training, mentoring or additional resources, to help the employee succeed

The aim of performance management isn't to punish. It's to give the employee every opportunity to succeed in their role while holding them accountable. It's a chance to ensure that the goals and standards of the role are crystal clear and that the employee has the tools and support they need to meet those standards.

It's really important to make it clear to your underperforming team member that performance management is a serious step. If there's no improvement within the agreed timeframe, it can lead to bigger actions, like formal warnings or even termination. That's why it's crucial to loop in

HR early, stick to your company's policies and keep good records of everything.

When handled the right way, though, performance management can be a game changer. It gives employees a clear plan to improve and shows you're being fair, consistent and holding everyone accountable across the team.

Effective performance management starts with clear and measurable goals. Employees should know exactly what is expected of them and how their success will be measured. These goals should be aligned with the overall objectives of the team and the organisation. Scan the QR code below for a template outlining a PIP:

Consider the case of Michelle, a client of mine who managed a sales team in a competitive retail environment. She noticed that one of her team members, Jake, was consistently underperforming. Rather than waiting for the annual review, Michelle decided to address the issue immediately. She set up a meeting with Jake, where they reviewed his sales targets and identified the barriers he was facing. Together, they developed a plan that included weekly check-ins, additional training and a mentorship programme. Over time, Jake's performance improved significantly, not only meeting but exceeding his targets.

The goal is to create a continuous feedback loop where employees feel supported and guided, with an end goal in mind that can be clearly reached and measured.

Honesty is also a critical aspect of performance management. By being upfront and transparent about performance issues, you save time and avoid unnecessary confusion. When employees know where they stand and what is expected of them, they can focus on meeting their goals rather than second-guessing their performance.

It's also important to recognise and address any patterns of underperformance. If an employee is consistently falling short despite support and guidance, it may be necessary to escalate the issue. Documenting these instances is essential, as it provides a clear record of the employee's performance and the steps that have been taken to address it.

It Might Be Time to Let Someone Go

Letting someone go is one of the most challenging aspects of management. It's a decision that should never be taken lightly and must always be approached with care, compassion and professionalism.

EXHAUST ALL OTHER OPTIONS FIRST

Before considering termination, make sure every other avenue has been explored. This includes:

- setting clear and measurable expectations

- providing regular, constructive feedback

- offering resources or support, such as training, mentoring or additional check-ins

- documenting all conversations, performance issues and the steps taken to support improvement (performance management)

It's also important to follow legal procedures to ensure fairness and compliance with employment laws. For example, in the UK, employees are entitled to a fair process, which may involve formal warnings, PIPs and the opportunity to address concerns. Check your organisation's HR policies and consult with your HR team to ensure you're following the right process. For international readers, employment laws vary, so it's essential to research and follow the regulations in your country.

With that in mind, letting someone go is deeply contextual and undeniably challenging. It's often overlooked in management books, likely because, truth be told, no manager has truly mastered it. It's not something we enjoy doing – in fact, it's something we instinctively want to avoid. But that's exactly why it's so crucial to have these discussions openly, whether in books, on podcasts or in leadership training. The more we talk about it, the better equipped we are to handle it with care and integrity.

HOW TO APPROACH THE CONVERSATION

One of the first times I had to let someone go was incredibly tough. We were both emotional, and it escalated quickly. Conflict arose during the meeting, I wasn't properly prepared and it ended in confusion and tears on both parts. Looking back, I realise how crucial it is to manage your own emotions before stepping into that room. While this moment will always be harder for the employee than it is for you, it's still undeniably difficult as their manager. That's why it's essential to approach the conversation with emotional awareness and solid preparation.

Now, I make sure I'm fully prepared and have the support I need beforehand. When it comes to the actual process of letting someone go, preparation is key. Here are some best practices to follow:

- **Be clear and direct.** Start the conversation by explaining the decision clearly and concisely. Avoid sugar-coating the message or getting into unnecessary debates. For example: 'We've had ongoing discussions about [specific issue] and, despite the support and feedback provided, there hasn't been enough improvement. Unfortunately, we've made the decision to end your employment.'

- **Show compassion.** Acknowledge that this is a difficult moment for the employee. Use language that conveys empathy while remaining professional. For example: 'I know this is not the outcome you wanted, and I want to assure you this decision wasn't made lightly.'

- **Offer support.** Provide practical support to help them move forward. This might include severance pay (if applicable), a reference or resources for finding new opportunities. If your company has an employee assistance programme (EAP), share that information as well.

WHAT HAPPENS NEXT?

After the conversation, ensure the process is handled with dignity:

- **Communicate with the team.** Be transparent with the remaining team members, without breaching confidentiality. For example, you might say: 'I want to let you know that [employee's name] is no longer with the company. This was a difficult decision made after careful consideration, and I'll be available to answer any questions or concerns you have.'

- **Rebuild trust and morale.** Terminations can impact team morale, so it's important to reassure the team and refocus on the future. Highlight the steps you're taking to ensure the team has the support it needs moving forward.

- **Document everything.** Make sure all paperwork is completed and records are updated. This ensures the process is compliant and there's a clear record for HR and legal purposes.

Letting someone go will never be easy, but with preparation, compassion and clear communication, it's possible to handle the process in a way that is fair and respectful to everyone involved.

Navigating Conflict with Confidence

I would like to make it clear that I've never had a difficult conversation go badly *when I've approached it the right way*. I've had to face some of the most awkward and tricky confrontations, covering both work-related and personal issues. But when I've come to the table with kindness, clarity and a genuine intention to help, nobody – *and I mean nobody* – has ever walked away wishing I hadn't told them the honest truth.

Now, I'll be real with you: there have been times in the past when I've handled these conversations poorly, either because I wasn't prepared, let emotions get in the way or avoided the issue for too long. And yes, those didn't always end well. But those experiences taught me the value of planning, empathy and staying focused on solutions.

These conversations strengthen your relationships, deepen trust and bring you closer together. If, however, the honesty you bring to the table exposes a divide and ultimately creates more distance, having the conversation is still the right thing to do – it brings clarity, sets boundaries and ensures that toxic behaviour doesn't go unchecked.

Challenge and disagreement in business is not only valid, it's extremely valuable. Watch out closely for how people take negative feedback or challenge well. Keep those people close.

Challenge and negative feedback (as long as delivered with kindness) should never further a divide. It should make you collectively stronger.

All you have to ask yourself is: *Would you want to know if your leader or peer was disappointed with your performance or didn't think you were working to your company's values? Or would you prefer they kept it quiet?*

Exactly.

Be kind. Never, ever ignore those difficult conversations.

And once you've had the tough conversations, the next challenge is making the right calls, and helping your team to do the same.

Stop Making Decisions

I once read the story of Adam Del Deo, Netflix's director of original programming at the time, who went to the 2017 Sundance Film Festival to look for new films to bring to Netflix's growing platform. Adam was captivated when he first saw *Icarus*, a thrilling documentary that unveiled the shocking doping scandal within competitive cycling. The film had just made waves at the festival, earning standing ovations and glowing reviews. It had all the makings of a game changer, and Adam was convinced it belonged on Netflix. But there was a catch: acquiring *Icarus* was going to be incredibly expensive – more expensive than any documentary Netflix had ever bought at the time.

Uncertain about whether to proceed, Adam looked to his boss, chief content officer Ted Sarandos, for advice. But Ted didn't give Adam the answer he was hoping for. Instead of deciding for him or pointing towards a certain direction, Ted said, 'If you believe this is "the one", go for it. But if you're not sure it's a game changer, don't overpay.'

Adam paused to take in Ted's words. The decision was his to make, no question about that, but the way Ted framed it gave him a clearer sense of how it fit into Netflix's bigger picture. Ted's point about asking whether the film was truly a 'game changer' shifted Adam's perspective. It wasn't just about his personal excitement, he needed to align with Netflix's goal of delivering bold, unique content without risking the financial strategy. Ted wasn't telling him what to do, but his input made it clear: this was Adam's call.

Confident that *Icarus* was worth the gamble, Adam gave the green light and placed a substantial bid. This moment became a defining one, both for Adam and Netflix, as *Icarus* not only won the Academy Award for Best Documentary Feature, but it became a phenomenon, ultimately winning the Oscar for Best Documentary Feature in 2018. Adam's decision paid off, and Netflix solidified its reputation in backing bold, thought-provoking content.

This story highlights one of Netflix's core leadership principles: 'Lead with context, not control.' Ted's refusal to dictate the decision wasn't a lack of support; it was instead an intentional choice to empower Adam. By providing the right context instead of micromanaging, Ted helped him build his decision-making confidence, a skill that would serve him, and Netflix as a business, tremendously well in the future.

Years later, the American author and professor, Erin Meyer, took to writing an entire book unravelling the fascinating story of Netflix's success. In her book, co-authored with Netflix co-founder Reed Hastings, *No Rules Rules: Netflix and the culture of reinvention*, she writes: 'The benefit of this [lead with context, not control] approach is clear – the person making the decision develops the muscle to make better independent choices down the line.' Netflix's strategy is simple: empower employees to take ownership of high-stakes decisions by giving them the information they need and the trust to execute them. Even when millions of dollars are on the line, it's not those in charge who make the call, but the people closest to the information.

This passage of what is a much-loved book for me, reminds me of a situation I encountered a few years ago. I had a brief but eye-opening conversation with the CEO of one of the world's largest technology companies. He was someone I deeply admired for his leadership style, so while I had his company across a meeting room table one day, I knew I wanted to take the opportunity to learn, so I asked him a quick-fire question while I had the chance: 'What's the biggest decision you've ever had to make?'

His response caught me completely off guard: 'I very rarely make decisions. My team are far more skilled than I am – that's why I hire them.'

I was stunned. Like most of us, I'd always assumed that decision-making was the ultimate responsibility of the leader – the final stamp of approval on everything important. Yet, his response, which I now know to be entirely aligned to Netflix's approach, showed me once again that great leaders don't hoard decisions. They instead stay away from making them and empower those around them to make the final call.

That conversation with the CEO planted a seed, but, I'll be honest – it took time to fully sink in. Back then, I was still caught up in the belief that being a good leader meant having all the answers and making every big decision myself. I thought my role was to be across every detail, weigh up every outcome and, ultimately, give the final yes or no on everything that mattered.

Looking back now, I can see how that mindset clashed with something I later embraced: the idea of playing to your strengths and not trying to master it all. In Rule #9, we spoke about leaning into your unique strengths rather than chasing after your weaknesses, and soon after my encounter with the CEO, I began to see how that applied to leadership decisions, too. It wasn't just about knowing my own strengths, but also trusting and empowering others to bring theirs to the table.

That shift didn't happen overnight, but it completely transformed how I approached leadership – and it all started with that one conversation. As I started to reflect more on what that CEO had said, I realised that holding on to all the decision-making wasn't a sign of leadership strength – it was a sign of control. And that control was holding me and my team back.

I saw it in the way people brought problems to me, waiting for my answer rather than offering their own solutions. I saw it in their hesitation to take risks or push projects forward without my input. The more I stayed in the centre of every decision, the more I became a bottleneck – and the more I realised I was creating dependency, not empowerment.

The real turning point came during a pivotal project in my career. We were launching an entirely new product. Every team in the business was involved, from engineering to marketing, and I was leading the whole thing. We had to move fast, and the success of the launch was critical to our business. At first, I felt such a need to control every detail that I stayed right in the thick of it, trying to approve every decision and stay on top of all the details. I'd done everything from giving the marketing team a list of social posts to create, to creating a list of features we needed in the new product for our engineering team to build. But, despite my best efforts, progress slowed – I was being invited into every meeting (and saying yes) and I started to see the tasks with 'Heather approval' on them building up. The team was stuck, waiting on me.

I had two choices: continue as I was – exhausted and making every call. I'd have to work into the night to get the team the approvals they needed. Or, take a leap of faith. Step back, give the team the context they needed and just let them run with it.

Nervously, I chose the latter.

I'd spent the weekend anxious about deadlines, so first thing Monday morning, I gathered the team, took some time to explain the bigger picture, why this project was so important for the business, our overall aim and where our North Star needed to be.

From there, I gave them the trust and autonomy to make decisions without me. I asked them to stop inviting me into meetings unnecessarily and explained that I had full confidence in their ability to make decisions. I made it clear that even if those decisions weren't always perfect, as long as we used them as learning opportunities, they would still have my full backing.

That didn't mean I disappeared entirely or stopped tracking progress. Instead, I focused on being intentional about how I stayed in the loop. I set up those regular check-ins we looked at in Rule #10 to create space for updates and feedback. These conversations gave me a clear picture of developments without undermining their autonomy.

Instead of hoarding responsibility, I shifted to being a guide. I offered clarity on our goals and priorities where needed, shared insights or resources if they were stuck, but left the *how* entirely in their hands. This balance allowed them to grow while ensuring I stayed connected to the bigger picture.

As with everything, there were a couple of weeks of messiness, people not feeling completely at ease with making the decisions at first. But one day, our head of engineering came to me and said, 'I decided we're going to remove the button feature you requested. When looking at our client feedback, the team noticed they don't actually want or need that extra button, and it will only reduce the usability of the product.'

I was a little taken aback at first, but very quickly felt awash with a huge sense of pride. They were right. Of course they were right. They were the closest to the problem. They had the right information to make the right decision. And they'd made it at speed.

Over the next few months up to launch, the team flew. They moved faster, made smarter decisions and brought solutions to the table I never could have considered.

Letting go of decision-making also meant I was focused on the right things: leading with vision, supporting the team when they needed it and stepping in at my best (only when absolutely necessary).

Like Netflix's philosophy of 'Lead with context, not control', empowering others to own decisions builds stronger, more capable teams and frees up us leaders to focus on what really matters.

The Illusion of Control

If you've ever found it difficult to let go and let your team make decisions without your input, you're not alone. We're hardwired to believe that if we're not directly involved in every choice, things will go wrong. Psychologists call this the 'illusion of control' – a cognitive bias that leads us to believe we have more influence over outcomes than we actually do.

This concept was introduced by psychologist Ellen Langer in her seminal 1975 paper, 'The illusion of control', published in the *Journal of Personality and Social Psychology*. In one of her experiments, participants were asked to buy lottery tickets. Some were allowed to choose their own numbers, while others were given random, pre-selected tickets. Later, both groups were offered the chance to sell their tickets back. Interestingly, those who had chosen their own numbers consistently demanded a much higher price to sell their ticket, despite the odds of winning being the same.

As part of her research, participants were asked to throw dice in a game of chance. They believed they were more likely to roll a high number if they threw the dice themselves, compared to someone else throwing it for them – even though the outcome was completely random and they couldn't influence the result whatsoever. Langer's study revealed a powerful insight: people feel more confident and more in control when they're directly involved in a process, even if their involvement has zero impact on the outcome. Now think about how this plays out in leadership.

When you're the one making decisions, it feels like you're reducing risk. You're the one steering the ship, so, naturally, you believe you're increasing the odds of success. But in reality, this hands-on approach can backfire. By holding on to decision-making, you're often increasing the risk, not reducing it.

As leaders, we're often removed from the front line. We see the big picture, the budgets, the deadlines and the stakeholder pressures, but we don't have the same hands-on knowledge as the people working on the details every day.

Imagine a busy restaurant kitchen. The head chef is in charge, but they can't see or hear everything that's happening at once. The servers know what the customers are asking for, the cooks know how long the food will take and the dishwashers know if they're running out of clean plates. Each person has a piece of important information that the head chef doesn't have. If they make every decision without listening to the team, things will fall apart. But if each team member is trusted to make decisions based on what they know – like the server deciding to hold off taking any more orders or the cook adjusting the timing to keep the food hot – the restaurant will run much more smoothly.

The head chef *feels* in control if they're making all the decisions, but they're relying on incomplete, second-hand information. The servers, the cooks and the dishwashers – *they* have the real-time data. They know what's happening, what's working and what's not.

When leaders insist on making every decision, they often make assumptions based on what they think is happening rather than what's actually happening. Those assumptions can lead to poor outcomes.

Let's say you're working on a major product launch like I was. Your team has been in the weeds for weeks – talking to customers, testing prototypes, refining ideas. You have a high-level view of the project, but you haven't been as close to the details.

Now, the team comes to you with two potential directions. You *could* make the call, relying on your broad understanding of the business strategy. But, if you do, you're inserting yourself into a decision based on second-hand information. Or, you could trust the team. They've done the research, they've gathered the insights and they're the ones who've built relationships with customers. They're closer to the problem and better equipped to make the decision. In that moment, it might feel risky to hand over control. But, in reality, it's far riskier to make a decision based on assumptions, without the full picture.

I've learned the messy way that the more I let go, the better my team performs. When I step back and empower those closest to the problem to make the decisions, they step up. They own their work, they take accountability and they're more invested in the outcome.

> *The illusion of control tells us that leaders need to be involved in everything. But true, empowering leadership isn't about holding the reins on every decision – it's about providing context, empowering your team and trusting them to make the right call.*

And only when we break free from the illusion of control can we build a team that's more engaged, more capable and far more confident in their own work.

The Trap of Decision Fatigue

By now, you've probably noticed a theme: letting go of decision-making isn't about avoiding responsibility – it's about making sure the right people are empowered to make the decisions instead. But there's another incredibly important reason why leaders need to stop making so many choices: decision fatigue, a concept we touched on in Rule #9.

The truth is, our brains aren't designed to handle endless decisions. The more choices you make in a day, the more your ability to make good ones deteriorates. Even small, seemingly insignificant choices (like whether to approve a report, respond to an email or adjust a meeting agenda) chip away at your mental energy. And when that energy runs out, you don't only start to slow down – you start making worse decisions.

That's why understanding decision fatigue is so important. You need to protect your capacity to make the decisions that really matter. If you burn through your mental reserves on every little choice, you won't have the clarity or focus needed for the big ones.

Psychologist Roy Baumeister found that our mental energy for making decisions is limited. Every decision – whether it's a high-stakes call about a business strategy or a minor choice about what to eat for lunch – depletes our cognitive resources. His groundbreaking research on decision fatigue is best illustrated through a study on judges and parole decisions, conducted in 2011. The researchers analysed over 1,100 parole rulings made by 8 judges in courts over a 10-month period. The results were striking:

- At the start of the day, judges were far more likely to grant parole, with favourable decisions made in about 65 per cent of cases.

- But as the day went on, the likelihood of granting parole dropped significantly – to *almost* 0 per cent before breaks like lunch.

- After a break, the likelihood of a favourable decision would reset, climbing back to around 65 per cent.

It wasn't the case details that determined the outcome – it was the time of day. Judges became mentally fatigued as they made more and more decisions, causing them to default to the easier, safer choice of denying parole.

Picture this: you're a creative director at a busy digital marketing agency. Your team's juggling a ton of projects, and one big client has just asked for point-of-sale materials for multiple countries. It's a massive task – different formats, different markets and endless tweaks to get everything just right.

At first, you're all over it – checking every design, reviewing fonts, layouts and colours for each region. But, as the deadlines pile up, you start cutting corners. Instead of letting your team own the process, you take over, making quick calls like, 'Just use the same layout for all the countries' or, 'Stick to the main brand colours – it's good enough.'

It feels like you're getting stuff done, but those snap decisions? They come back to bite you. The designs don't quite hit the mark for certain regions, the client isn't thrilled and now there's extra work to fix it all. This is what happens when decision fatigue kicks in. It's easy to go for the quick wins, but those shortcuts can cost you in the long run.

How to Find the Balance

Letting go of decision-making feels uncomfortable, especially when you're used to being the one who steps in to solve problems and make the final call. But the truth is, in order to level up and become a great leader, we can't be making every decision. We must set the context, coach our teams and empower them to take ownership at every opportunity.

Here's how to shift from decision-maker to context-setter:

GIVE CLEAR CONTEXT (AND LET GO OF THE REST)

When someone comes to you for guidance, don't jump straight to the solution. Instead, give them the bigger picture they need to make their own call. Think about the goal, the risks and any non-negotiables. Then move out of the way and let them align their decision with that context.

For example, imagine your team is deciding whether to launch a new feature now or delay it for further testing. Instead of saying, 'Launch it,' give them the context:

- 'Our goal is to improve customer retention.'

- 'The risk is that we launch too early and create a bad user experience.'

- 'We need to stay within the existing budget.'

With that information, they can make an informed decision, rather than relying on your stamp of approval.

ASK QUESTIONS, DON'T SOLVE PROBLEMS

When a team member asks for your input, resist the urge to give an answer. Instead, guide them to find it themselves by asking thoughtful questions that encourage critical thinking.

For example, suppose a marketer comes to you and asks, 'Should I focus on social media or email marketing?' Instead of choosing for them, ask:

- 'Which platform is performing better right now?'

- 'Where is our target audience more engaged?'

- 'Do you feel confident in both areas or is additional training needed?'

These questions help them analyse the situation and build their decision-making muscle. Over time, they'll come to you with solutions instead of problems.

CHALLENGE BIASES

As managers, we like to think we're making rational, well-informed decisions. But the reality is, we all have cognitive biases that cloud our judgement. These mental shortcuts can cause us, and our teams, to overlook important information, misinterpret data or make decisions based on assumptions rather than facts.

Two biases that show up *a lot* in management are:

1. **Confirmation bias: the 'I knew it all along' trap.** Confirmation bias is the tendency to seek out information that confirms what you already believe and ignore evidence that challenges your views. Essentially, you're looking for proof that you're right, instead of trying to see the full picture. Let's say you've got a team member who's convinced a certain marketing strategy isn't working. They might cherry-pick data to back up their belief, ignoring any evidence that suggests the strategy is actually improving. Confirmation bias can also show up during performance reviews. If you *already* believe someone on your team is underperforming, you're more likely to notice and remember their mistakes while overlooking their wins.

2. **Selection bias: the 'recent = relevant' fallacy.** Selection bias happens when we put too much weight on recent events or data points and assume they're representative of the bigger picture. We focus on

what's immediately in front of us, rather than stepping back to consider the full context. Imagine your team is discussing how well a product launch went. If they're only looking at the most recent customer feedback (say, the last month's worth), they might assume the product is performing poorly, when, in reality, the overall trend shows steady improvement. Selection bias also creeps into hiring decisions. Managers might overvalue a candidate's most recent job performance without considering their long-term track record. Or they might overreact to a single mistake a team member made last week, instead of evaluating their overall contributions.

Your job in decision-making is to help your team see beyond these biases and make more well-rounded decisions.

For example, if someone on your team says, 'We should double down on social media because our last post went viral,' challenge that thinking:

- 'Are we basing this on one success or is there a consistent trend?'

- 'What other data do we have that supports this decision?'

This helps them avoid snap judgements and dig deeper into their reasoning.

OFFER EXPERIENCE, NOT DICTATES

When your team is stuck, it can be helpful to share your own experiences. But be careful – don't frame your advice as the only way forward. Instead, offer it as one perspective and encourage them to think through their own options.

For example, you might say, 'Here's what happened when I faced a similar situation, but different people and circumstances can lead to different outcomes.' This approach shows that you trust their judgement and want them to build their own confidence, rather than relying on your past experiences as a blueprint.

PROVIDE THE SAFETY NET

Empowering your team to make decisions doesn't mean we can abandon them. Make it clear that you're there for support if things go sideways. But don't swoop in at the first sign of trouble – give them space to work through the problem first.

For example, if a team member is worried they've made the wrong call, respond with:

- 'I trust you to handle this, but let me know if you need a second opinion.'

- 'What's your plan to fix it if things don't go as expected?'.

- 'I know you have got this, but if it doesn't work out, we can always fix it together.'

By creating a safety net, you give your team the confidence to take calculated risks, knowing they're not alone if things go wrong.

ENCOURAGE DECISIONS MADE FROM ABUNDANCE, NOT FEAR

One of the biggest blockers to decision-making is fear: fear of failure, fear of judgement, fear of things going wrong. This is backed by psychology – when we make decisions from a place of fear, we activate our amygdala, the part of the brain responsible for processing threats and triggering the 'fight, flight or freeze' response. When the amygdala takes over, our ability to think rationally and creatively is compromised. We narrow our focus to avoiding risk, which limits our capacity to explore options, innovate and make balanced, thoughtful decisions. Instead of thinking, *What's possible?* we get stuck in *What could go wrong?*

Psychologists call this 'loss aversion', another cognitive bias that makes us more focused on avoiding losses than on gaining potential rewards. According to research by Daniel Kahneman, author of *Thinking, Fast and Slow*, people feel the pain of loss twice as strongly as they feel the joy of gain. This fear of loss often drives people to avoid taking risks altogether, leading to indecision or overly cautious choices.

As a leader, we need to be aware of this and try to spot it in our team. Then make them aware, and encourage them to actively move away from making decisions from a place of fear, and instead from a place of abundance.

For example, ask questions like:

- 'Are you solving a real problem or one you're afraid might happen?'

- 'What would this decision look like if you were coming from a place of trust?'

- 'What would you do if you knew you couldn't fail?'

This reframing helps them move beyond defensive thinking and focus on the best possible outcome.

Why This Works

By letting go, you're not losing control – you're breaking free from the *illusion* of control.

When you trust your team to make decisions, they feel more ownership over their work. They'll be more invested in the outcomes, more willing to take risks and more motivated to solve problems without waiting for your input.

So, next time someone comes to you with a problem, pause before you step in. Ask yourself: *Am I giving them the context they need to succeed or am I holding on to control out of habit?* Shift your mindset, ask the right questions and watch your team step up in ways you never expected.

We've explored the power of stepping back and letting your team take ownership of decisions. Now, let's focus on how you communicate in those moments. Because the way you step back matters just as much as the act itself.

Rule #13

Talk Like the Boss

When I got my first couple of management roles, I failed – a lot – when it came to communication. I was paranoid about saying the wrong thing at the wrong time. I second-guessed every email, stumbled through meetings and never quite knew when to speak up or stay quiet. Far from coming across as confident or competent, I felt like I was constantly fumbling my way through, just hoping my team wouldn't see how out of my depth I felt.

I still vividly remember one meeting early on. I'd called the team together to brainstorm ideas for a new project. Instead of letting the discussion flow, I kept jumping in, trying to steer every conversation. I was so focused on making sure we didn't go off track that I ended up shutting people down. The result? A few polite nods, some awkward silences and a team that left the room feeling uninspired. I remember walking away thinking, *What just happened?*

Fast-forward a few years, and things couldn't have been more different. By then, I'd worked alongside some of the greatest managers in the game – multi-million-pound business builders, FTSE 100 CEOs and even the guy who built Microsoft Excel (yes, really). I started noticing patterns in how these leaders communicated. They didn't dominate conversations or micromanage interactions. They asked thoughtful questions, listened deeply and created space for others to contribute. I began writing down what I observed, refining those patterns and putting them into practice.

I'll never forget another meeting with a different team, years later. This time, instead of trying to control everything, I opened the discussion with a clear goal, asked open-ended questions and let the team take the lead. When I did speak, it was to guide or clarify, not to dictate. The energy in the room was completely different: people leaned in, ideas bounced around and we left with an action plan the team was genuinely excited about.

That shift didn't happen overnight, but it transformed me into a confident and powerful communicator without losing my authenticity. My team respected me more, my meetings became productive (and even enjoyable) and I felt more in control.

That's why I'm so passionate about sharing what I've learned here.

Communication is no longer just a 'soft skill'
that can be brushed off. It's a critical part of
leadership that separates the good from the great.

Whether you're sharing a new idea, resolving a conflict or checking in with your team, the way you communicate can make or break your success. And to be clear, the communication I'm covering in this chapter isn't just about talking – it's about truly understanding people: what motivates them, what worries them and what they need to thrive. It's about building trust through active listening, asking thoughtful questions and showing genuine care for their perspectives.

Great communication also means knowing when to coach, when to influence and when to step back. It's about creating a sense of clarity and purpose so your team knows exactly where it's headed and how to get there. This isn't surface-level; it's about connection, collaboration and inspiring action.

But before we dive into how to talk like the boss, it's important to first look at some of the common communication pitfalls I see.

Common Communication Traps

Imagine this: you're part of a team led by Amanda, a manager who's always rushing to provide answers. During meetings, she jumps in before anyone's finished their thought, over-explaining ideas to the point where the team tunes out. She means well, but her quick responses and dominating approach leave little room for others to contribute. Over time, the team starts holding back. They don't feel heard, ideas stop flowing and resentment quietly builds. The result? A disengaged team and a manager left wondering why no one seems motivated anymore.

Or take another example: Carlos, a manager who's great at setting goals, but rarely follows through on his commitments. He tells his team he'll advocate for their ideas to senior leadership, but never quite gets to it. Slowly but surely, the trust erodes and people stop bringing him their best ideas because they don't believe he'll follow through.

These are just two examples of the five most common communication pitfalls managers face:

1. **Talking more than listening.** Managers often dominate conversations, failing to actively listen to their team's ideas or concerns.

   - **Impact**: Employees feel unheard and creativity and collaboration are stifled.

2. **Not following through.** Making promises or commitments (for example, 'I'll escalate this' or 'We'll address this soon') and then not delivering.

   - **Impact**: Trust erodes and employees become disengaged or hesitant to share ideas.

3. **Assuming everyone understands.** Failing to confirm clarity after meetings or instructions, assuming the message has been understood.

   - **Impact**: Miscommunication leads to errors, wasted time and missed expectations.

4. **Being too vague or indirect.** Delivering unclear messages or avoiding specifics to dodge confrontation or conflict.

   - **Impact**: Employees are left confused about priorities, leading to inefficiency and frustration.

5. **Responding too quickly.** Reacting impulsively to issues or concerns without fully understanding the situation.

   - **Impact**: Quick responses may overlook key details, leading to poor decisions and unresolved conflicts.

In this chapter, I'm going to show you how to move away from these traps and give you everything you need to know about communication as a manager – whether you're leading a meeting, resolving a conflict, or simply trying to get your message across without second-guessing yourself.

How to Talk Like the Boss

Let's face it – a few of you lucky ones out there are naturally amazing communicators, but, for the rest of us, we don't enjoy speaking in front of crowds and the thought of commanding a room can feel overwhelming. We're never taught how to communicate effectively as managers; we've been left to figure it out as we go, usually learning through trial and error. But here's the good news: great communication isn't about being the loudest or most outgoing person in the room. It's a skill and, like any skill, it can be learned and refined.

In this section, we'll break down communication into four key areas to help you talk like the boss:

1. **One-to-one communication:** Building trust and clarity in your personal interactions.

2. **Communicating within your team:** Leading meetings and guiding team discussions.

3. **Communicating across the business:** Establishing credibility in cross-departmental conversations.

4. **Public speaking:** Commanding a room and establishing yourself as a thought leader.

These habits have transformed how I lead, and I know they'll do the same for you. From meetings to everyday interactions, we're about to dive into how you can communicate like the boss.

ONE-TO-ONE COMMUNICATION:
STOP TALKING, START LISTENING

Active listening is one of the most important skills a leader can have – it can completely change the dynamic of a team. In fact, Gitnux's Active Listening Statistics and Trends report in 2023 found that managers trained in active listening saw a 30 per cent boost in employee satisfaction, and team collaboration and productivity shot up by 25 per cent. And yet, so many leadership training programmes focus on the outward stuff – like public speaking or presentation skills – while listening gets left in the shadows.

So what is active listening? It's the practice of giving your full attention, understanding the message (and the feelings behind it), responding thoughtfully and remembering what's been shared. It sounds simple, but it's not always easy, especially when you're busy or distracted.

Imagine this: a team member comes to you with a concern about a project. If you're practising active listening, you'd stop what you're doing, close your laptop, focus on them and really hear them out – without jumping in or offering a quick fix. You'd confirm what they've said to make sure you're on the same page and then work together to find a solution.

Now compare that to brushing them off or half-listening while thinking about your next meeting. That's why practising active listening skills is a must for any leader who wants to build a strong, connected team.

A FEW TIPS TO IMPROVE YOUR LISTENING

- **Write it down.** Even if it's just a casual chat, have a pen handy. Jotting down notes helps you remember key points and keeps you engaged in the conversation. That said, balance is key – you don't want to be so focused on writing that you lose the personal connection. Instead, jot down quick keywords or phrases to capture the essentials, and make sure to maintain eye contact and use verbal cues like 'I see' or 'That makes sense' to show you're actively listening. If it's a longer or more formal conversation, you can say something like, 'This is really helpful – do you mind if I jot a few things down so I don't miss anything?' It shows respect for what's being said and keeps the interaction natural.

- **No devices in meetings.** This one really frustrates me. When you bring a laptop or phone into a meeting, it creates a visible divide between you and your team. Even if your intention is just to take notes or keep an eye on things, the message you're sending is that something else might take priority over the conversation in the room.

  Now, I get it – some people might push back. Is it okay to have your phone face down on the table? Personally, I think it's still distracting. Even if you don't pick it up, it acts as a mental pull. Your focus isn't entirely on the people in front of you because part of your mind is still wondering if something's lighting up that screen.

  That said, I'm not unrealistic. Life happens. If you've got kids in school or elderly parents to care for, it's perfectly fine to communicate your boundaries upfront. Say something like, 'I usually don't bring my phone into meetings, but I've got an important call I'm keeping an ear out for. If something comes up, I'll step out.' This way, you're showing respect for the team's time while being transparent about why your device might need to be accessible.

The bottom line? Being fully present sends a powerful message: you value your team's time and input. Emergencies aside, most things can wait until the meeting's over. And if you're worried about taking notes, use pen and paper instead – it's less intrusive and keeps the focus where it belongs: on the conversation in the room.

- **Stay curious.** Ask questions to dig deeper. When you show genuine interest in someone's opinion or idea, it builds rapport and helps you understand their point of view more thoroughly.

In a world full of distractions, giving someone your full attention is a rare and valuable skill. There is a huge opportunity to stand out just by doing this alone. But it's more than just being polite . . . When leaders truly listen, they send a clear message: *What you're saying matters*. This helps people feel heard, valued and respected, which is the foundation of psychological safety.

In environments where psychological safety exists, people are more likely to speak up, share ideas and admit mistakes without fear of judgement. Great leaders who master active listening create this kind of culture, where team members feel confident that their voices will be respected, no matter their role or perspective, building trust and creating a space where people feel safe to contribute fully.

Silence speaks volumes

We often think that great leaders are those who have all the answers, fill every silence and fix every problem right away. But, as we saw in the previous chapter, that's not true. In fact, knowing when to stay silent can be just as important as knowing when to speak. Pausing in conversation allows others to contribute and shows that you're open to their thoughts. It also gives you time to reflect on your own response, making your communication more thoughtful and considered.

Great leaders know when to stop talking and just listen. Here's what they do differently:

- **Say 'I don't know'.** It's okay not to have all the answers. In fact, admitting that you don't know something builds trust. People appreciate honesty and humility far more than a leader who pretends to know it all.

- **Resist the urge to fill silences.** Awkward pauses are fine. Let them happen. They often encourage deeper thinking and better responses from your team.

- **Give others the spotlight.** Sometimes, the most powerful move is stepping back and letting others have the floor. You don't need to jump in on every conversation – besides, the more you contribute, the more work you pile onto your plate. It's perfectly fine to sit out some discussions.

Slowing down your responses in all the ways above and embracing the silence creates a space where real communication can happen. Everyone gets a chance to shine, and trusts that you'll make space for them. It shows your team that you value their input, and it helps you make better decisions.

COMMUNICATING WITHIN YOUR TEAM: KEEP YOUR WORD

We live in a world where social media filters and unrealistic standards of success are everywhere, making trust feel like a rare commodity. Surrounded by polished images and empty promises, it's no surprise that people are left sceptical about what's genuine – and who they can rely on. Gallup's State of the American Manager report found that only 13 per cent of employees strongly agree that their managers are effective at building trust. But by prioritising transparency and consistently keeping our promises, we have a great opportunity to rebuild that trust and break through the scepticism. Trust is earned not through the words we say, but by holding true to those words, consistently delivering on even the smallest of promises.

Keeping your word as a manager is one of the simplest yet most powerful ways to build trust with your team. That trust doesn't just shape your relationships – it can completely define your career. When you consistently follow through on your promises, it sets you apart as someone reliable and credible. But when you don't? That's when things can start to go wrong.

There's a psychological concept called 'social exchange theory' (SET) that explains this beautifully. The theory, first developed by George Homans in the 1950s and later expanded on by Peter Blau, suggests that relationships are a bit like transactions. We're always weighing up what we're giving and what we're getting in return. When the exchange feels fair, trust grows. When it doesn't, doubts creep in.

If you break a promise as a manager, it can throw off that balance entirely. Your team might feel undervalued or start to think that their trust in you isn't being reciprocated. The same research into SET has shown that, when trust is damaged, it's much harder to repair, and it can lead to all sorts of issues in teams, like disengagement and resentment.

On the flip side, consistently keeping your word creates a positive cycle. It builds trust, respect and credibility, not just in the eyes of your team, but in the way you're perceived as a leader across the company. So, every promise you make is a chance to reinforce that trust and set yourself apart. By upholding your word, whether it's about career development or day-to-day tasks, you create a team that trusts you and feels confident in your leadership.

It's important to recognise that doing what you say you're going to do isn't just about following through. It's also about being honest and transparent when you can't.

Here are some practical examples of how to build this trust, showing you'll always do what you say you're going to do with your communication as a leader:

1. **Handle professional progression chats with care.** If someone on your team asks about a promotion or raise you can't promise, don't just give them vague answers or try to please them in the moment by promising

anything you can't follow through with. Be upfront about what's realistic and give them a clear path forward: 'I can't promise a promotion in the next few months, but I want to help you get there. Let's focus on [specific goals or skills], and we'll set up regular check-ins to track your progress.'

This way, you're being honest while showing you're invested in their growth, even if the timing isn't perfect.

2. **Address workload overflow from other teams.** When another department piles tasks on one of your team members that fall outside their core responsibilities, it's important to protect your team while keeping the bigger picture in mind. For example, you might say:

'I know this extra work isn't in our remit, but I also understand how critical it is. Let's discuss how we can fit this in without compromising your priorities, and I'll have a conversation with the other team to make sure this doesn't become a recurring issue.'

By acknowledging the burden while actively finding solutions, you demonstrate fairness and advocacy for your team. This gives you and your team space to follow through on commitments, by ensuring you don't overcommit on things that aren't a priority.

3. **Back up promises with action.** When you make a commitment – no matter how small – follow through and come back to the person or team involved. For example, after helping an employee secure a training opportunity they requested, let them know: 'I just approved the training course you asked about, and you should receive an email confirmation soon. Let me know if there's anything else you need.'

These small acts of follow-up not only demonstrate reliability, but also strengthen your reputation as someone who takes their word seriously.

By using these practical approaches, you'll build a culture of trust where your team knows they can count on you, not one that is fed up of empty promises. Leaders who consistently deliver on their promises create teams that trust them. And when your team trusts you, they're more willing to follow your lead, even when times get tough.

A big part of maintaining that trust is how you communicate, especially during meetings . . .

COMMUNICATING ACROSS THE BUSINESS: COMMUNICATING WELL IN MEETINGS

When leading meetings or guiding team discussions, clarity is key. Many managers fall into the trap of over-explaining or jumping into solutions too quickly, leaving their teams disengaged or confused.

- **Start with a clear agenda.** Outline what you're here to achieve. For example, 'Today, we need to decide on the project timeline and assign responsibilities.'

- **Facilitate, don't dominate.** Ask open-ended questions to encourage input. For example, 'What are your thoughts on this approach?' or 'What challenges do you see with this plan?'

- **Stay on track.** If the conversation drifts, bring it back with phrases like, 'Let's revisit the original question.'

> ## TIPS IF YOU'RE NERVOUS ABOUT LEADING MEETINGS
>
> 1. **Prepare in advance.** Write out key points or questions you want to cover.
> 2. **Start small.** Practise running smaller, low-stakes meetings before taking on larger ones.
> 3. **Remember, you don't have to have all the answers.** Your job is to guide the discussion, not solve every problem on the spot.

PUBLIC SPEAKING: PRACTISE CONFIDENCE IN YOUR VOICE

Speaking in front of a room, whether it's a team meeting or a conference, can be daunting. But public speaking is one of the most powerful tools for establishing credibility as a leader.

A lot of us struggle with confidence when we communicate, especially in leadership roles. When I first started in management I'd sit in meetings with people who seemed to articulate themselves so effortlessly. They'd speak with this air of confidence and clarity, and I'd think to myself, *I could never be like that.* It felt like they had some secret skill I didn't. But here's what I've learned over time: confidence in your voice isn't something you're born with – it's something we can practise and build. And one of the best places to start is with your writing.

Start with written communication

Written communication is one of the easiest ways to practise being clear, concise and confident in how you express yourself. Writing forces you to slow down and really think about what you want to say and how you want to say it.

Steven Bartlett, entrepreneur, podcast host and investor, shared an eye-opening insight in his episode of *The Diary of a CEO* with Daniel Priestley. He explained that his ability to articulate himself so clearly, tell compelling stories and communicate with impact is a skill he attributes to a practice he calls his 'single biggest life hack': writing one tweet every day.

Bartlett described how this daily habit forced him to refine his thoughts, strip away the fluff and focus on clarity and impact. It was this ruthless, daily pursuit of concise communication that transformed the way he expresses himself. For managers, this lesson is gold. Writing is a practice that sharpens your ability to articulate ideas effectively. It teaches you how to get to the heart of the matter, frame your message in a way that resonates and leave a lasting impression. Whether it's drafting an email, preparing a presentation or even jotting down your thoughts in a journal, writing helps you practise the kind of clear, confident communication that leadership demands.

When you write, you're essentially rehearsing your thoughts. You're structuring ideas, organising your points and refining your message in a way that speaking doesn't always allow for in the moment. This process strengthens your ability to get to the heart of what matters, and that's a skill you'll naturally carry over into conversations, meetings and presentations.

Plus, writing can be edited. You can go back, adjust your tone, cut out anything unnecessary or even rearrange your points for clarity. Editing helps develop the habit of choosing your words carefully, which boosts your confidence when you're speaking because you've already trained yourself to focus on what matters.

Here's when this works really well:

- **High-stakes conversations**, like giving feedback, pitching an idea or addressing a tricky topic. Drafting your thoughts in writing first can help you feel more prepared.

- **Defining your message.** If you're unsure how to articulate something clearly, start by writing it down. It'll help you figure out what you really want to say.

TIPS FOR BUILDING CONFIDENCE IN YOUR WRITING

If writing feels like a challenge, start with these three simple tweaks:

1. **Cut the filler words.** Words like 'just', 'I think' or 'I believe' are ways of us softening our message. You're already saying it, so it's clear you think or believe it!

For example, instead of:

→ 'I think we should move forward with this plan.'

Try:

→ 'We should move forward with this plan.'

Or instead of:

→ 'I just wanted to check if this works.'

Try:

→ 'Does this work?'

It's direct and confident.

2. **Keep it concise.** After you write an email, try cutting it down by half. This is a great exercise to force yourself to say only what's necessary. Clear and concise messages show confidence – and save everyone time.
3. **Stop over-apologising.** Apologies have their place, but they lose impact when overused. Instead of saying, 'Sorry for the delay', you could say, 'Thanks for your patience.' It's subtle but shifts the tone towards confidence and appreciation.

When you practise confident communication through writing, it naturally builds your confidence when you speak. Why? You're less likely to second-guess yourself in the moment because you've already worked through the 'what' and 'how' of your message. Over time, you'll find that clarity and authority come to you much more easily, whether you're writing it down or saying it out loud.

PRACTICAL TIPS FOR PUBLIC SPEAKING

- **Start strong.** Open with a hook – a story, statistic or question that grabs attention.
- **Keep it simple.** Focus on two to three key messages and repeat them throughout. Don't overload your audience with too much information.
- **Speak with intention.** Slow down, pause for effect and vary your tone to keep people engaged.
- **Practise relentlessly.** Record yourself, rehearse with a friend or even practise in front of a mirror. The more you practise, the more natural it will feel.

Great Communication Is a Skill, Not a Talent

At the heart of great communication is clarity, whether you're leading a meeting, making a decision or presenting an idea. It's not about being the loudest or most charismatic person in the room; it's about being the one who listens, brings people together and inspires action.

Start small. Pick one of these areas to focus on this week – maybe it's improving how you listen to your team or practising how you wrap up decisions in meetings. With time and intention, you'll transform the way you communicate and, in turn, the way you lead.

But great communication isn't just about how you speak – it's also about what you're setting people up to achieve. Because no matter how well you articulate your vision, your team can't deliver if they don't know what success actually looks like. Clear expectations, measurable progress, and shared accountability – this is where KPIs come in.

Understand KPIs (and Empower Your Team to Actually Hit Them)

Let me take you back to 2003. At Amazon, the company was scaling at breakneck speed. Jeff Wilke, head of Amazon's Worldwide Consumer business, was overseeing warehouses full of stock and a logistics chain that was struggling under growing demands. The company's KPIs – delivery speed, inventory accuracy and efficiency targets – seemed almost impossible to achieve as Amazon stretched to meet the needs of an expanding customer base. Wilke understood that for Amazon to sustain its growth, they couldn't simply put arbitrary targets in place and hope people would push to meet them; they needed a culture where every team member was genuinely motivated to achieve these KPIs.

To make this happen, Wilke introduced Amazon's now-famous 'Ownership' principle, which emphasises that employees should act as though they own the business – taking responsibility for outcomes, thinking long term and going beyond their job descriptions to drive success. This mindset aimed to weave accountability towards these KPIs throughout the fabric of the company, from how teams ran their meetings to how new employees were hired.

In fact, it became so central to Amazon's DNA that it even reshaped the hiring process. Interviewers no longer just looked for skills; they sought out candidates who embodied this sense of ownership. They wanted people who wouldn't just do the job, but would take pride in driving the company forward, naturally feeling accountable for achieving their goals.

In KPI reviews, the ownership principle was a game changer. Team members weren't asked to simply report on numbers, they were encouraged to ask themselves why performance was lagging and, most importantly, what they could do to fix it. It gave everyone a role in growing the business from the ground up. Instead of feeling like bystanders, employees were empowered to bring solutions to the problems they saw around them. By removing blame and excuses, accountability started to feel real.

The impact of this culture shift on Amazon's growth and operational excellence was incredible. This principle helped Amazon both reach its KPIs and build a culture where employees felt truly invested in the company's success.

In this chapter, I'll walk you through practical, real-world steps to make KPIs more meaningful and achievable for your team. Together, we'll look at ways to inspire your team to aim for these goals, celebrate wins along the way and create a shared sense of accomplishment. Whether you already have KPIs given to you from the business that you need to delegate to your team or you're building them yourself from scratch, this chapter will be your guide to building a solid set of KPIs and getting your team to actually care about hitting them.

What the Hell Are KPIs?

Let's start with the basics. Key performance indicators, or KPIs, are metrics designed to show how well a team or organisation is progressing towards its big goals. Think of them as the dashboard indicators on a car: without them, you'd have no idea how fast you're going or if you're low on fuel. KPIs help organisations navigate and stay on course, transforming broad goals into smaller, concrete steps. However, KPIs often feel abstract, intimidating and even useless, especially if they're set without a clear purpose or we're constantly unable to hit them. A well-thought-out KPI does much more than set a target; it turns success into something tangible and meaningful.

Back when I was managing GoProposal, we had a set of KPIs that didn't exactly resonate with everyone on the team. One instance that stands out was our copywriter and SEO expert. Her main metric was simply reporting on the number of people landing on our blog each month. The numbers she brought every month were accurate, but they didn't reflect the actual value of her work or give her a chance to really showcase the creativity and strategy she brought to the table.

Realising this, I decided to get her reporting on more than just numbers. Alongside blog traffic, we added prompts like, 'What have you been testing or working on this month that's really clicked?' and, 'What hasn't worked out as expected, and what might you do differently?' This small shift gave her the space to share her successes, challenges and experiments – going beyond a figure on a page. It meant she could shine in front of her peers, showing both the creative and analytical sides of her work alongside the data. This approach made her KPIs more meaningful and inspired her to keep pushing boundaries, knowing her effort was genuinely seen and valued by the team each month.

Let's look at Apple for another example. As a former COO with a focus on operational excellence, Tim Cook reshaped Apple's supply chain by shifting the focus of its KPIs. Instead of only tracking 'units shipped', Apple's metrics began addressing questions like, 'How quickly are customers receiving their products?' and 'How satisfied are they with the experience?'

These new qualitative KPIs highlighted customer satisfaction as a core metric, giving Apple a unique advantage and shaping what we know as their impeccable customer experience today. Apple's approach shows how a thoughtful KPI framework can help a company to truly prioritise the right outcomes by going beyond numbers on a spreadsheet.

Here are two primary types of KPIs that we need to use in our teams to ensure we feel inspired to actually hit them:

1. **Quant**-itative KPIs: These are numerical metrics that quantify success. They include figures like growth, speed and cost. For example, measuring the percentage of on-time deliveries provides concrete data on logistical performance.

2. **Qual**-itative KPIs: Unlike quantitative metrics, qualitative KPIs capture less tangible elements of success, such as customer satisfaction or employee morale. These metrics reflect how people feel about an experience or product, which can be just as critical to success as hard data.

When KPIs are thoughtfully balanced between quantitative and qualitative, they become more than mere numbers. They tell a growth story, encourage motivation and make team members feel part of a bigger mission.

Like Tim Cook's Apple and the copywriter at GoProposal, teams that embrace this dual approach can see their KPIs not just as metrics, but as drivers of meaningful, sustained progress for the team.

But here's the catch: for KPIs to genuinely drive progress, each team member needs to know exactly where they fit into that picture. Imagine this: your team is reviewing last month's numbers, only to find that the KPI for new customers was missed by 20 per cent. As you discuss what went wrong, it becomes clear that no one's entirely sure who was responsible for generating leads, following up on prospects or even finalising conversions. Without clear ownership, KPIs like these can easily fall through the cracks – everyone assumes someone else is handling it, but, ultimately, no one is accountable. It's time to discuss clarity in roles.

Clarity in Responsibility

There is a dangerous psychological concept that's vital for us to understand here, known as 'the diffusion of responsibility'. This phenomenon shows up in group settings and states that people are *less* likely to take responsibility for an action (or inaction) when they can assume someone else will handle it. In a workplace, this can look like team members sitting back on tasks or KPIs, believing someone else will step up. It leads to delays, missed targets and a lack of accountability.

For us managers, it's crucial to be aware of this concept. If everyone on the team thinks responsibility is shared, there's a good chance no one feels fully accountable, and it's here that diffusion of responsibility quietly but powerfully undermines KPIs. Imagine you're in a team meeting, discussing a recent KPI miss. As you look around the room, it's clear that no one is quite sure who was responsible for what. This scenario is a familiar one in teams without clearly defined roles and responsibilities for the individuals in that team. When ownership is vague, results suffer – everyone thinks someone else is taking charge of pushing towards a KPI, but, ultimately, no one feels accountable.

We want to flip that on its head by ensuring that each person has clearly defined KPIs. This means we can eliminate that ambiguity, giving each team member clarity over their personal stake in the outcomes. When KPIs are assigned individually, they become more than just group numbers – they're a *personal* commitment, which makes people far more likely to drive them upwards.

In practical terms, assigning three to five specific KPIs to each person does wonders to counteract the diffusion of responsibility. When team members know precisely which results they're responsible for, they're far less likely to assume others will pick up the slack. Instead, they'll feel empowered to own those outcomes, which drives their engagement and proactive problem-solving. Then, when things do go off track, it's much easier to identify who needs support, rather than conducting a team-wide search for answers.

Managers who actively counter diffusion of responsibility create teams that are sharper, more engaged and highly accountable. A 2023 study by the Society for Human Resource Management (SHRM) found that teams with clear role and KPI definitions reported a 50 per cent higher employee satisfaction and a 32 per cent reduction in turnover. This correlation between role clarity and retention illustrates why clear roles are foundational to KPI success – when employees know their responsibilities well, they're not only more satisfied, but also more likely to stick around and deliver on their KPIs. The clarity helps to turn KPIs from abstract numbers into meaningful drivers of personal and team success.

Even in a company as vast as Google, where personal KPIs might seem impossible to manage, the introduction of OKRs – objectives and key results – made individual accountability achievable and highly effective. They are a standout example of how to create personal accountability within a massive organisation.

Introduced in 1999 by John Doerr, the OKR framework has transformed Google's approach to goal-setting by making responsibilities transparent and measurable. OKRs became Google's blueprint for creating a culture where each person's role is clear and every goal is visible across the organisation. Each team member's objectives are aligned with company-wide goals, with specific, measurable KPIs (or 'key results') attached to each objective. This approach keeps the company aligned and directly combats the diffusion of responsibility that can easily arise in large organisations.

So, what exactly are OKRs and how can you use them?

SET OBJECTIVES

Objectives are the 'what' – they're clear, ambitious goals that you want to achieve. Think of them as the destination you're heading towards. They should be inspiring and meaningful, something that challenges your team and aligns with larger company goals. For example, an objective for a product team might be: 'Deliver a market-leading user experience.'

CREATE KEY RESULTS

Key results (KRs) are the 'how' – they're measurable steps or KPIs that show you're progressing towards your objective. KRs are specific, time-bound and measurable, providing a clear way to assess if the objective is being met. Each object-ive typically has three to five KRs attached to it, making them concrete and actionable. For our product team example, KRs could be:

- 'Reduce page load time by 0.5 seconds by Q4.'
- 'Achieve a 15 per cent increase in user engagement by the next quarter.'
- 'Reach a user satisfaction score of 90 per cent by year-end.'

Objectives are shared across the team, but the KRs are differ-ent for every individual.

COLLABORATE ON THE METRICS

Start by asking each team member to set their OKRs at the start of a quarter (or project cycle) and schedule a meet-ing with them to discuss their OKRs to ensure that they are aligned with team and company priorities. This gives your team ownership over their goals and gives you an opportunity to think strategically with them. OKRs are typically reviewed every month or quarter to assess progress and change if necessary.

This can be seamlessly integrated into your 90-day 1-on-1s (see Rule #10), ensuring that goal-setting is a structured, strategic conversation rather than a one-off exercise. By embedding OKRs into these regular check-ins, you create a rhythm of accountability and alignment while giving your team the space to refine their goals over time.

SHARE YOUR GOALS

OKRs work best when they're visible across the organisation, allowing everyone to see how each team member's work aligns with the broader goals. This transparency combats diffusion of responsibility by clarifying exactly who's responsible for each KR. If a KR is falling short, it's easy for everyone to identify where the company needs additional support or new solutions to get back on track.

By setting ambitious objectives and clear, measurable KRs, OKRs create a culture of ownership. Each team member knows exactly what they're working towards, how it aligns with the company's vision and how they'll measure success. This practical structure allows even large organisations like Google to maintain clear accountability and ensure that each person's contributions drive real impact.

Google's consistent success in meeting ambitious targets can be traced back to the clarity, alignment and accountability embedded in its OKR framework. This model has since been widely adopted, with countless companies using it to prevent diffusion of responsibility and foster a culture where individuals feel genuinely accountable for the organisation's overall success.

To keep momentum and ensure those KPIs actually stay on track, we need to regularly revisit our goals and hold people accountable to progress – this is where structured meeting rhythms come in.

Far from being just another annoying slot blocked in the calendar, these meetings will become an essential tool to keep KPIs visible, track progress and offer support where needed. When set up thoughtfully, they transform KPIs from static numbers into dynamic, team-wide drivers of success.

Let's dive into how to create meeting rhythms that reinforce accountability and keep your team aligned with their KPIs.

Meeting Rhythms: How to Structure KPI Accountability

LinkedIn offers a great example of how to invest in meeting rhythms designed for KPI accountability. Every year, LinkedIn holds an 'InDay' – a company-wide day for employees to align on goals and refocus their efforts. Then, throughout the year, LinkedIn uses monthly team KPI reviews and quarterly in-depth meetings to stay on track. These sessions go beyond basic check-ins. Each monthly meeting requires team members to present their KPI progress, discuss challenges and share solutions. The result? A transparent, high-accountability environment where everyone feels connected to the company's larger mission.

Effective meeting rhythms balance regular touchpoints with the flexibility to adapt. Here's an example of an ideal structure:

1. **Biweekly 1-on-1s:** Regular 30-minute check-ins for personal goal discussions and progress updates. (We discussed these in Rule #10 – these are the same 1-on-1 sessions that are there to 'hold space', but they can also be used to offer support on KPIs where needed.)

2. **Monthly team KPI review:** A one-hour session where the full team comes together to review their individual KPI performance and shares insights.

3. **Quarterly deep dive:** Every third team session, extend the meeting to a two-hour session to assess broader strategies and tackle complex challenges together.

4. **Annual reset day:** A day-long alignment session to revisit goals and reframe priorities. Scan the QR code below to get my full agenda for this session:

This cadence is inspired by high-performing teams like those at Netflix and LinkedIn, where clear, consistent meeting rhythms are seen as essential to achieving KPIs. A well-structured meeting rhythm provides a balance of support and accountability, enabling teams to stay on track without feeling micromanaged.

USING THE MEETINGS TO DIG DEEPER

Imagine a KPI review where team members bring not just their latest metrics, but also insights on what worked, what didn't and, most importantly, what's next. This approach doesn't happen by accident – it's the result of asking the right questions to create accountability.

Sheryl Sandberg was known for her relentless focus on probing questions during her time at Google. Her approach inspired teams to think critically and take ownership of their metrics. By asking questions that went beyond the data, Sandberg created a culture of inquiry and accountability.

Research supports the effectiveness of this approach. A study published in the *Journal of Management Studies* found that leaders' questioning behaviour was significantly associated with increased team learning and improved performance. The reason? Open-ended questions force people to think, reflect and take ownership.

How we frame these questions is important for ensuring that they energise and empower the team. Questions like 'What's the data?', 'Why are we here?' and 'What are we doing about it?' empower team members to take control of their KPIs. Instead of feeling evaluated, they feel supported and encouraged to bring insights and solutions to the table. This shift from directive to inquiry-based leadership can transform KPI discussions into collaborative problem-solving sessions.

Language that empowers rather than instructs creates a sense of ownership. Consider an employee who's struggling to meet their KPI for lead generation. A directive approach might sound like: 'Why don't you try following up more frequently?' While this is a reasonable suggestion, it subtly shifts accountability to you, the manager, because you're providing the solution.

Netflix's Reed Hastings emphasises the power of reframing language to promote independent thinking. In his book *No Rules Rules*, he discusses leading with context rather than control. Instead of giving direct instructions, he asks his team open-ended questions that encourage them to develop their own strategies. For instance, he might reframe the earlier directive to: 'What strategies can we test to increase lead generation next month?', empowering employees to take ownership of their goals.

This language shift keeps the responsibility with the team member and creates a more accountable environment by asking them to propose solutions. Hastings' approach is a reminder that even small changes in language can have a profound impact on how KPIs are perceived and pursued.

But accountability alone isn't enough. For team members to truly push their limits and innovate, they need to feel secure in taking risks. This brings us to the next essential element: psychological safety – the foundation that allows individuals to pursue challenging KPIs without fear of failure.

Psychological Safety: An Essential Ingredient for Reaching KPIs

As we discussed in Rule #5, psychological safety is a fundamental element in building a high-performing team. It's the shared belief that team members can speak up, take risks and make mistakes without fear of punishment or humiliation. When psychological safety is present, team members feel free to innovate, share openly and grow – essentials for reaching ambitious KPIs.

Just as we push our limits in the gym to build strength, growth in the workplace also requires a willingness to risk failure. I discussed in Rule #5 how, in the gym, my goal is to reach the point of muscle failure, beacuse I'm looking for as much growth as possible – and I've brought this same mindset into leadership. For our teams to achieve significant KPIs, they must be able to push boundaries without fearing repercussions. This freedom to experiment allows them to set ambitious targets and tackle big challenges head-on.

But psychological safety doesn't happen on its own: it's something we have to consciously create and protect. In the context of KPIs, it's particularly important because, without it, team members may only aim for safe, easy-to-achieve goals rather than stretching towards impactful, ambitious ones.

Here are a few practices that will help reinforce a psychologically safe environment as your team works to hit their KPIs:

1. **Build failure into KPIs.** Alongside metrics, encourage a focus on experimentation. Ask questions like, 'What are we testing this month?' and 'What didn't work, and what have we learned?' These conversations normalise setbacks and make it clear that failure is part of the process, ultimately empowering the team to aim high and reach further.

2. **Seek out rejection.** Growth-driven KPIs mean striving for big wins, which inevitably involves some rejection. Encourage your team to pursue opportunities that may

not always go smoothly; if every answer is 'yes', then the stretch isn't big enough. Use the tool we looked at in Rule #5 when we explored how to encourage failure in your team – embrace and log rejections as steps towards success, reinforcing that failure is part of the journey to ambitious targets (see page 86).

3. **Try 'bad ideas only' brainstorming sessions.** In brainstorming sessions, use 'bad ideas only' as a rule to force out-of-the-box creativity. This approach makes it safe for everyone to contribute, often leading to breakthrough ideas while reinforcing that every suggestion has value, even if it seems unconventional.

As we align on KPIs, it's vital to remember that achieving these goals isn't just about the numbers. A culture of psychological safety allows your team to take calculated risks, push their limits and ultimately reach ambitious targets. Embracing failure isn't just about growth; it's often the driving force behind your team's biggest successes. So, as you focus on KPIs, revisit whether your team feels safe to fail – this could be the key to unlocking their full potential.

A KPI-Driven Culture

The stories from the greats – Amazon, Microsoft, Apple and Google – teach us a valuable lesson: if we want a team that truly cares about KPIs, we must build a culture of accountability, curiosity and resilience. This means creating an environment where team members feel empowered to innovate, responsible for their outcomes and supported in pursuing ambitious goals.

A KPI-driven culture thrives when roles are clear, meetings are purposeful and conversations build ownership, much like LinkedIn's InDays or Microsoft's streamlined approach to meetings. With the right structures in place, KPIs become a powerful tool for growth and achievement, transforming daunting targets into goals that genuinely inspire pride and progress within your team.

In the next chapter, we'll explore accountability in more depth – what it truly means to hold ourselves and our team accountable, and how to build the systems and habits that make it possible. By embedding these principles into your leadership, you can create a foundation where KPIs drive real results and push your team to achieve greatness.

Use Accountability to Turn Goals into Action

Accountability is the foundation of every successful team. It's the ability to take ownership of actions, results and decisions. But while it's a critical ingredient for achieving those KPIs we looked at in the last chapter, accountability remains one of the most misunderstood concepts in leadership.

Too often, accountability is seen as a tool for blame – a way to point fingers when something goes wrong. But, in reality, accountability is about building a team where all members feel empowered to take responsibility for their work and are motivated to deliver results (even when things go wrong). It's less of 'Who's at fault?' and more of 'How do we keep moving forward?'

Forbes reported that 80 per cent of managers struggle to hold their teams accountable effectively and 91 per cent of employees say accountability is one of the most important leadership skills missing in their workplace. The consequences of a lack of accountability can be severe:

- **Missed goals.** Without a culture of ownership, teams are less likely to hit their KPIs.

- **Low morale and disengagement.** When accountability is absent, work can feel directionless, leading to frustration and apathy.

- **Erosion of trust.** Commitments are broken and trust between team members and leaders begins to deteriorate.

On the flip side, when accountability is done right, it creates alignment, fosters trust and drives performance. It's the secret weapon for ensuring your team not only understands their KPIs, but actively works to achieve them.

In this chapter, we'll explore how you can build a culture of accountability that empowers your team to take ownership of their results. You'll learn practical strategies to shift accountability from being a source of stress to becoming a driving force behind your team's success – and the success of your KPIs.

But before we get deep into the practicalities of accountability, we need to understand its greatest enemy: blame.

The Negative Impact of Blame

Blame in leadership is a corrosive force that undermines team performance, morale and accountability. When leaders point fingers instead of owning their role in challenges, they create a culture where individuals are more concerned with deflecting responsibility than solving problems.

One of the most destructive elements of blame is its ability to shift focus away from solutions. In a blame-driven culture, team members spend more time justifying failures or pointing to external factors than identifying ways to improve. A study by Culture Partners found that 82 per cent of employees either avoid holding others accountable or try but fail to do so. When blame becomes a default response, we stall progress and create an environment where excuses replace accountability.

A powerful example of blame's negative impact can be seen in the world of sports leadership. In a high-pressure environment like professional football, a coach who blames the players for every loss will create a fractured team dynamic. If a coach publicly criticises individual players without reflecting on their own tactics or decisions, it demoralises the team and shifts focus away from collective improvement. This behaviour creates a mindset where players are more concerned with not being scapegoated than with performing at their best. In contrast, successful leaders like Sir Alex Ferguson always took responsibility when things went wrong. Instead of blaming others, he focused on what the team could learn and how they could improve next time. In his book *Leading: Learning from life and my years at Manchester United*, he talks about how making this shift built trust and loyalty within his team. It's no surprise that this mindset played a huge role in creating one of the most successful football legacies of all time. By focusing on growth instead of blame, Ferguson created an environment where his players felt supported and motivated to do better.

In the corporate world, the consequences of blame can be even more far-reaching. A lack of accountability often creates confusion about who is responsible for what, which allows excuses and finger-pointing to thrive. When no one truly understands their role or objectives, missed targets become opportunities for blame rather than lessons for improvement.

Let's look at an example: imagine a sales team that fails to meet its monthly revenue target. The manager blames the marketing team for not generating enough qualified leads, while the marketing team points to product issues as the real problem. With no clear accountability, the focus shifts away from solving the underlying issues and on to defending personal performances. The result? No clarity, no progress and a cycle of frustration and missed goals.

Blame directly contributes to this lack of clarity because it distracts teams from determining where responsibility truly lies. Instead of clearly defining roles and addressing root causes, blame shifts the conversation to finding fault. The Culture Partners study found that 93 per cent of employees felt unclear about their company's objectives and unable to align their work with broader goals due to a lack of accountability. Without clarity on who is accountable for what, blame becomes a convenient escape route, further deepening the lack of alignment.

Blame is toxic to leadership. It prevents teams from focusing on solutions, erodes trust and stifles innovation. Accountability, on the other hand, creates an environment where both successes and failures are owned and addressed constructively. Leaders who focus on building accountability create stronger, more resilient teams that learn from setbacks instead of becoming paralysed by them.

Blame may offer short-term relief for a leader's ego, but it will always undermine long-term success. Without accountability, businesses face inefficiency, low morale and stagnation – while a culture of accountability drives clarity, trust and progress.

In the next section, we'll explore how you can create a culture of accountability that inspires your team to take ownership and stay aligned with your organisation's goals.

From Blame to Accountability:
The Mindset Shift

Having an accountability mindset is crucial for leaders. It means owning the outcomes of your team's efforts, even when the cause of failure may not have been your fault originally. Whether it's a missed deadline caused by poor communication, an external challenge like supply chain delays or a lack of clarity around roles, effective leaders don't waste time pointing fingers. Instead, they step up, assess what went wrong and focus on solutions.

For example, let's say a product launch is delayed because another department didn't deliver their part of the project on time. While it's easy to blame the other team, that doesn't actually solve anything or move us forward. Instead, strong leaders recognise that their role is to ensure alignment and clarity across departments. They own the outcome by asking, 'What could I have done differently to prevent this?' and 'How can we make sure this doesn't happen again?' Owning the problem doesn't mean accepting fault – it means taking responsibility for moving forward.

I once worked with a team leader who was struggling to get her team to take responsibility for their performance. Deadlines were being missed and KPIs were falling short daily. Despite raising these issues with her team repeatedly, nothing seemed to change.

Seeking advice, she approached me. As we talked, it became clear that she hadn't realised one crucial detail: she herself was frequently late to meetings and often failed to follow through on her own commitments. Her actions, unintentionally, were setting a poor example for the rest of the

Just because something isn't your fault doesn't mean it's not your problem.

team. I asked her a simple question: if she wasn't demonstrating accountability herself, how could she expect her team to follow suit?

Accountability starts with the leader. Once she embraced this and began modelling the behaviour she expected from her team – being punctual, meeting her own deadlines and taking responsibility for her work – things began to shift. Although, the transformation didn't just happen because she set a good example; it also required intentional coaching and practical adjustments. She began having regular conversations with her team to reinforce expectations and align everyone on what accountability looked like in practice.

This example highlights how powerful leading by example can be, but it also shows the importance of pairing it with supportive structures like clear expectations, regular feedback and coaching. Leadership behaviour sets the tone, but it's the systems and conversations that truly embed accountability into the team's culture.

Accountability must be ingrained in a team's culture, and it starts from the top. Leaders need to set clear expectations, ensure that roles are well defined and establish systems that promote transparency and responsibility. Research shows that organisations with high leadership accountability tend to perform better. For instance, McKinsey's 'State of Organizations 2023' report identifies leadership accountability as one of eight key factors driving positive work-related outcomes.

HOLDING OUR TEAMS TO ACCOUNT

Holding team members accountable means creating a world at work where they feel supported to take ownership over their daily actions. Let me paint a picture with two very different approaches to accountability: the typical blame game versus a coaching conversation:

The blame game

Manager: 'This isn't good enough. We're not hitting our KPIs and you're letting the team down. Why didn't you hit your target? You need to sort this out, or we'll be having a very different conversation next month.'

Team member's reaction: They feel defensive, maybe even a little defeated. Inside, they're probably thinking: 'I'm already trying my best – what else do they want from me?' or, worse, 'Fine, I'll do what I can, but I'm done putting in extra effort.'

What happens next? Not much. The team member keeps doing the same thing they've been doing because there's no trust or support to try something new. They avoid taking risks, and the cycle repeats next month. The team member feels deflated and you're still stuck with the same issues.

The coaching conversation

Manager: 'Let's chat about last month. You didn't quite hit your target of 30 leads – what do you think happened?'

Team member: 'I was focusing on email and LinkedIn outreach, but I wasn't getting much response. And then LinkedIn went down for a day, so I lost momentum.'

Manager: 'That's frustrating. So, those methods didn't work out – what else are we trying next time?'

Team member: 'Maybe I could try cold calls or tweak my email strategy. I could also check in with [colleague] – they seemed to do well this month.'

Manager: 'That sounds great! Let's set up a mid-month check-in to see how those ideas are going and adjust if we need to. I know you've got this – let's figure out what works best together.'

What happens next? Instead of feeling criticised, the team member feels supported and, as a result, more motivated. They leave the conversation with a clear plan and a sense of ownership over the solution. They're now more likely to try new approaches because they know you've got their back and you're invested in their success.

By swapping blame for a coaching mindset, you build trust and inspire ownership. Instead of shutting people down and demotivating them, you open the door to creativity and growth, and help them to see challenges as opportunities for growth.

Accountability done right is about lifting people up, helping them grow and making sure they have the tools and confidence to try new things, setting them up to deliver next time.

Accountability in Reporting

A key component of building accountability is establishing a structured reporting system. This means creating a process where both quantitative and qualitative performance is reviewed (see page 241 for a reminder of the difference between the two). Numbers tell part of the story, but it's equally important to assess the quality of the work and the strategies behind it. As we learned in the last chapter, leaders should encourage their teams to analyse why things went wrong and, more importantly, follow up with actionable solutions. Accountability means owning the solution, not just identifying the problem.

For instance, instead of simply asking why performance lagged, ask:

- 'What factors contributed to this outcome?'

- 'What adjustments can we make to improve next time?'

- 'What support do you need to succeed?'

By framing the conversation this way, you help teams move beyond explaining the problem to actively owning the path forward.

To support this, regular KPI meetings should follow a clear and structured agenda that combines both numbers and insights:

1. **Headlines.** Share the key performance metrics (the numbers).

2. **Why.** Discuss the reasons behind success or failure (the analysis).

3. **What we're doing about it.** Outline next steps to address gaps and sustain progress (the accountability).

This structure ensures that meetings remain productive and forward-looking, rather than turning into sessions where teams simply explain away poor performance.

Without this proactive approach, many leaders fall into the trap of only providing feedback when something goes wrong. Research shows that 80 per cent of employees report receiving feedback solely in response to problems. This creates a negative feedback loop where employees begin to associate feedback with failure. Over time, this damages morale, reduces motivation and fosters a culture of avoidance – where employees feel discouraged from taking risks or being open about challenges.

Instead, encourage regular, constructive check-ins that focus on both progress and opportunities for improvement. These conversations should celebrate what's working and identify ways to build on that success, while also addressing gaps in a way that empowers the team. This aligns closely with the importance of everyday feedback, as we explored in Rule #10 – accountability isn't just about annual reviews, but about creating a rhythm of ongoing, candid conversations. This balanced approach keeps everyone aligned with their goals and accountable for their results while fostering a culture of trust and continuous improvement.

The Role of Feedback in Accountability

Feedback plays a critical role in building accountability. According to Gallup, nearly half of employees only receive feedback a few times a year, and only 26 per cent say that this feedback helps them improve.

When feedback is infrequent or unclear, it leaves team members feeling disconnected from their goals. They may start to question whether their efforts even matter or if their contributions are being noticed. Without regular feedback, accountability begins to crumble because employees aren't given the opportunity to understand where they stand or how to course-correct.

Imagine being told only twice a year that you're falling short on a KPI – it feels too late to fix anything and often leads to frustration or disengagement. Team members might think, *Why didn't anyone tell me sooner? I could've done something about it.* This lack of timely feedback discourages them from taking ownership because they feel unsupported and out of the loop.

To create a culture of accountability, feedback needs to be regular, constructive and focused on improvement rather than blame. Leaders should build a safe environment where team members feel comfortable discussing both successes and challenges. This ties directly back to Rule #10 – the foundation of accountability is everyday feedback, not just occasional performance reviews. It opens the door for honest conversations about what went wrong and how to fix it, rather than allowing the team to fall into the blame game.

When employees know that feedback is frequent and supportive, they feel empowered to take accountability for their results. They trust that their progress is being monitored in real time and that they'll be given the tools and guidance to improve. Regular feedback loops not only keep employees engaged and committed to their KPIs, but also foster a stronger sense of ownership and drive. It's this ongoing dialogue that transforms accountability from a top-down directive into a shared team mindset.

Accountability as the Ultimate Team Builder

In conclusion, accountability is not just a managerial tool – it's the glue that holds high-performing teams together. It starts with the leader, but it permeates through the team as each member takes responsibility for their work. When accountability is embedded in the culture, teams become more engaged, innovative and committed to achieving their goals. Leaders who master accountability, while balancing it with empathy and support, will cultivate teams that not only meet but exceed their targets.

But accountability alone isn't enough – teams also need the right focus. The next step is ensuring that energy is spent on the work that truly moves the needle.

Rule #16

Focus on What Matters

When Whitney Wolfe Herd founded Bumble in 2014, she was stepping into a crowded and competitive online dating market, dominated by established players like Tinder and Match.com. To succeed, Wolfe Herd knew she couldn't rely on throwing money or hiring at new problems – her competitors were doing that already. Bumble had to work smarter, not harder.

Whitney Wolfe Herd kept things simple. Instead of trying to do everything, she focused on one clear idea: giving women control in dating. She made sure her team worked on just this, without getting distracted by trends or adding too many features. The Bumble app was designed to be easy to use, with a clean look that didn't overwhelm people. Every choice – from how you swipe to the app's colours and branding – was about keeping it simple and empowering women. This way, the team's time and energy went where it mattered the absolute most.

In marketing, Wolfe Herd and her team used smart, low-cost ways to spread the word about Bumble. Instead of spending a lot of money on big ads, she asked students to promote the app at their schools and teamed up with social media influencers. This helped people hear about Bumble in an organic and relatable way. Remarkably, within just seven years of launching Bumble in 2014, she had built the company into a business worth £3 billion.

The company I worked at, GoProposal, faced a challenge back in 2019 that many growing businesses know all too well: limited resources. We had no external investment, a tiny team and no spare budget for flashy marketing campaigns or endless new hires. But instead of seeing these constraints as obstacles, we chose to view them as opportunities. These so-called 'positive constraints' became the foundation of our success.

As I described in Rule #4, while competitors with bigger budgets hosted extravagant events to woo potential clients, we organised intimate dinners for our existing clients, creating deeper relationships and cultivating loyalty. These small, thoughtful gatherings made a bigger impact than any high-ticket spectacle ever could.

Similarly, when it came to marketing, we couldn't afford expensive paid campaigns. So, we got strategic with organic social media, crafting engaging, authentic content that resonated with our audience. Every post, every interaction, was designed to maximise impact without spending a penny. By working smarter with what we had, we not only kept pace with our competitors, but carved out a unique space in the market.

The lesson here is universal: whether you control your company's budget or not, there's immense value in embracing constraints. The next time you hear, 'We don't have the budget to hire' or 'We can't afford that right now', let it be a call to get creative. Use the resources already at your disposal – your time, your ideas, your people – and work on getting them to operate smarter, not working harder.

*Often, the greatest innovations come
not from abundance but from necessity.*

Our role as their manager is to guide our teams towards what truly matters, ensuring time, energy and resources aren't wasted on pointless tasks. When I work with corporates today, I see the sheer volume of unproductive meetings, which often pull people away from deep, focused work. Add to that endless email threads, unclear priorities and poorly integrated systems, and it's no wonder teams often feel overwhelmed and directionless.

Asana surveyed over 10,000 workers from around the world for their Anatomy of Work Global Index and found that, on average, they spent 60 per cent of their time on activities that take time away from *actual* work. These activities included searching for information, switching between apps, managing shifting priorities and chasing the status of work. Over the course of a year, the average worker spent 103 hours in unnecessary meetings, 209 hours on duplicated work and 352 hours talking about work. The stats from Asana are pretty eye-opening. It's frustrating, and it leaves people drained and unmotivated.

This chapter is all about putting an end to that. I'm going to walk you through how to cut through the noise and how to focus better for your team. We'll talk about spotting inefficiencies, focusing your efforts where they make the biggest impact and building a team dynamic that's all about clarity, results and keeping people empowered. By the end, you'll not only have a better handle on your team's time and resources, you'll also create a work environment that feels productive, empowering and motivating for everyone.

Be the Guide

As a manager, think of yourself as the compass guiding your team. Each person brings unique strengths and skills, and your role is to channel their energies, allocate resources effectively and align them towards the goals that matter most. Even the most talented teams can become misaligned or overwhelmed without clear direction and structure.

Creating a cohesive and efficient team is about ensuring your team members have the time, space and tools to do their best work. This means building clarity around priorities, defining roles and making thoughtful decisions about how resources – time, energy and effort – are distributed. When done well, you create a team that moves in harmony, where each member knows what to focus on and how their contributions fit into the bigger picture.

In a landmark study, Asana sought to understand how employees in organisations spend their time. What they found was startling: up to 60 per cent of an employee's work-week is consumed by tasks that don't contribute to their core priorities. More than half of the week is spent on busywork like unnecessary meetings, overly long email threads or chasing approvals for tasks that could have been automated or streamlined.

Now, imagine what your team could achieve if even a fraction of that wasted time was redirected towards meaningful work. By creating a structure where priorities are clear, workflows are efficient and resources are optimised, you enable your team to operate at their full potential. It's not about turning your team into a 'well-oiled machine', but rather a dynamic, high-performing group where every effort counts and every resource is used thoughtfully to drive results.

Your job as a manager is to be the guide – to ensure the team's energy is focused on what matters most, eliminate unnecessary obstacles and create an environment where meaningful work thrives. By doing so, you don't just help your team succeed; you inspire them to bring their best to every challenge.

For one team McKinsey observed, the issue became painfully clear during a time audit. A manager realised their team was spending nearly ten hours a week preparing reports no one acted on. Another department discovered a recurring weekly meeting that ate up two hours of everyone's time, but consistently ended without decisions or actions. The implications of this inefficiency are enormous in both productivity and the frustration it creates for our teams who feel their skills are being underutilised.

For teams that took action, the turnaround was dramatic. One company simplified its meeting structure, cutting out all but the most essential, decision-focused sessions. Another automated repetitive tasks, saving hundreds of hours annually. By focusing on what truly mattered, these organisations not only freed up valuable time, but also saw a boost in morale and engagement as employees shifted their energy to work that made a real impact.

Time is your most valuable resource, and it's up to you as a manager to ensure it's being used wisely. The next exercise will help you do exactly that. It is a practical tool to eliminate wasted time and energy in your team. By mapping out each team member's tasks, you can identify overlaps, unnecessary meetings and tasks that don't add value. This clarity will allow you to streamline workflows, remove bottlenecks and cut out non-essential work, freeing up your team to focus on the areas where they excel and make the biggest impact.

Streamlining Your Team's Workload

One of the most impactful concepts I've taught in webinars and corporate training is helping managers identify and eliminate unnecessary tasks from their team's workload. The goal isn't to scrutinise or micromanage – it's about freeing up time, reducing stress and ensuring everyone can focus on meaningful, high-impact work. When teams are bogged down by unnecessary tasks, it's not just frustrating – it's a sure-fire way to overwork and burn them out.

But how do you pinpoint what's unnecessary without making your team feel like their work is under the microscope? Managing a team's workload effectively means focusing their energy on the tasks that matter most while reducing unnecessary effort. Here's a clear, collaborative three-step process to help you identify what adds value, what needs to change and how to create a more efficient, empowered team.

STEP 1: BUILD OUT ROLE AND RESPONSIBILITES DOCUMENTS

The first step is to get a clear picture of what your team is doing day-to-day. This is where the roles and responsibilities (RNR) documents come in.

Here's how it works:

1. **Ask your team** to create a detailed list of all the tasks they work on daily, weekly and monthly – not just

what's in their job descriptions, but what they're actually doing.

2. **Focus on reality.** Emphasise that this is not a performance evaluation. The goal is to gather insights on their workload and identify opportunities to work smarter, not harder.

Below is an example message to your team:

> Hi team,
> I know everyone's plates are full right now, and I want to focus on how we can work more effectively. Over the next two weeks, I'd like everyone to jot down a list of your daily, weekly and monthly tasks – don't worry about making it polished, just focus on capturing what you're spending your time on. Once these are ready, we'll meet to review and figure out where we can streamline or shift things to make your workload lighter and more impactful.

This step helps you gather the data needed to move forward while ensuring your team feels part of the process.

STEP 2: REVIEW AND CATEGORISE TASKS

Once you have the RNR documents, the next step is to evaluate each task collaboratively.

Understanding your team (20 minutes)

Start your 1-on-1 meeting by understanding how your team member feels about their workload and where they believe they add the most value. Some example questions include:

- Which tasks take up the most time in your day-to-day work?

- Are there any tasks you feel aren't a good use of your skills or could be done more efficiently?

- What parts of your role do you enjoy the most or feel the strongest at?

- Are there tasks that feel repetitive or unnecessary?

- If you had more time, what priorities or projects would you like to focus on?

This builds trust and ensures your team feels supported, not scrutinised.

Categorising tasks (20 minutes)

Now, work through their list together and sort their tasks into three categories:

1. **Core tasks.** These are the essential, high-value responsibilities that are critical to their role. These tasks directly contribute to team or organisational goals and align with their strengths. For example: preparing detailed project plans or delivering client presentations.

2. **Supportive tasks.** These are tasks that need to get done, but don't necessarily require as much focus. They might be processes that could be streamlined, delegated or made more efficient. For example: manually updating spreadsheets or scheduling internal meetings.

3. **Excess tasks.** These are tasks that add little value, take up unnecessary time or could be reassigned, automated or stopped altogether. For example: attending meetings with no clear purpose or writing overly detailed reports that aren't used.

STEP 3: STREAMLINE, DELEGATE AND REFOCUS

Once the tasks are categorised, it's time to take action. Collaborate with your team member to identify practical ways to streamline their workload:

- **For core tasks:** Find ways to help them focus more time and energy on these responsibilities. For example, remove distractions or offer additional support to help them excel in these areas.

- **For supportive tasks:** Explore options for delegating these tasks, automating processes or setting clearer boundaries around how much time they should take.

- **For excess tasks:** Work with them to stop doing these tasks or reassign them. For example, you could agree to reduce unnecessary meetings or replace manual reporting with an automated tool.

Below is an example conversation for supportive and excess tasks:

Manager: 'You mentioned that manually updating the spreadsheet each week takes a lot of time. Could we automate this or find someone else on the team who might be better suited to handle it?'

Team member: 'Yes, that would be great. I think the spreadsheet could be linked directly to our database to pull the numbers automatically.'

Manager: 'Perfect – let's look into that together. And for that weekly status meeting, would it be helpful if we switched to a quick email update instead?'

Team member: 'That would save a lot of time. I'd rather use that hour to work on client follow-ups.'

By the end of this process, you should have collaboratively reduced unnecessary tasks, freed up your team's time and created a clearer sense of purpose for their day-to-day work, working smarter and building a team that's focused, empowered and aligned with the goals that matter most.

A Manager's Blueprint for Smarter Work

Whitney Wolfe Herd's journey with Bumble is a masterclass in resourcefulness. By focusing her team's efforts on a single, clear vision – putting women in control of dating – she avoided the pitfalls of overcomplication. Every decision, from Bumble's app design to its marketing strategies, was guided by simplicity and impact. Her ability to eliminate distractions, streamline processes and direct resources towards high-value efforts turned Bumble into a $3 billion company, proving that smart, strategic work beats sheer effort every time.

The lessons from GoProposal align perfectly with this principle. When faced with limited resources, we chose to embrace our constraints as opportunities for innovation.

Intimate client dinners outperformed expensive events and carefully crafted organic social media content delivered results without a hefty price tag.

These lessons show that our greatest power lies not in doing everything, but in doing the right things. As the conductor of your team's orchestra, your job is to align each player's unique talents and ensure their time is spent where it makes the biggest difference. This chapter has provided you with the tools to do just that – giving you and your team a practical framework to declutter workloads and focus on what truly drives results.

Of course, this is an ongoing process. Quarterly check-ins will help you keep tasks aligned with evolving priorities and ensure your team remains agile in the face of change. These reviews are your opportunity to celebrate wins, recalibrate where needed and keep your team focused on meaningful goals.

Building a resource-conscious team gives them the clarity and capacity to focus on what they do best. You empower them to innovate, contribute meaningfully and feel proud of their work.

And with that, we've reached the final rule. Everything we've covered so far – from communication to accountability to focus – has led you here.

Your Boss Era Begins Now

So, here we are. You've made it to the end. Not just of this book, but of your mindset shift, your transformation in how you see yourself as a manager, how you approach your team and how you set yourself up for long-term success.

And if you take just one thing away from this book, let it be this: management cannot just be a title. It's a responsibility. A practice. A craft.

We don't just step into a role and instantly become great at it. No one does – not the best leaders you admire, not the mentors who've shaped you and certainly not me. Every great manager you've ever seen has had their moments of doubt, their failures and their tough decisions that kept them up at night. But what separates those who thrive from those who struggle is their commitment to learning – *and* to unlearning.

The 16 Rules That Shape Exceptional Managers

Throughout this book, we have explored the 16 fundamental rules that make a great manager, covering both skills for people and skills for systems. If you have been reading with an open mind, you will have noticed a theme running through every chapter: management is not about controlling people or being the smartest person in the room. It is about creating an environment where work is clear, expectations are fair, accountability is shared and people can do their best work.

You have learned how to handle difficult conversations in a way that builds respect rather than resentment. You now understand why psychological safety matters, not as a feel-good idea but as a foundation for innovation, trust and high performance. You have seen how clear KPIs – used well – can be a manager's best tool for driving results, and how account-ability is not about blaming but about creating ownership.

You have explored decision-making, prioritisation, dele-gation and how to balance long-term strategic thinking with the everyday pressures of managing a team. These are not just theoretical concepts. They are the real-life skills that sep-arate average managers from exceptional ones.

But knowledge alone does not make us great. You could read every management book in the world (I did a whole university degree on it), and it still would not prepare you for the day your best employee hands in their notice, or when you have to make a call on something without enough infor-mation, or when a project you have invested months into suddenly falls apart.

The difference is in the action.

Everything in this book means nothing if you close it now and go back to working the way you always have. But if you take even one idea from these chapters and apply it – if you start questioning your own habits, making adjustments, trying, failing and refining – you will already be so far ahead.

And that is the real challenge. Not just to read, but to commit.

Commit to having the difficult conversation you have been avoiding.

Commit to setting clear expectations, even when it feels awkward.

Commit to giving your team the autonomy to think for themselves, even when it would be easier to do it yourself.

Commit to being the kind of manager people remember, not because you were perfect, but because you made them feel safe.

If you are still reading, I want to say thank you – for investing in yourself and your team. Thank you for choosing to do the work of becoming a better manager rather than just hoping it will get easier with time. The fact that you picked up this book, read it and made it to the end tells me that you care, not just about your own success, but about the success of those around you.

That is why I wrote this book. Because when more of us understand how to manage well, more people get to love the work they do.

Work is such a huge part of our lives. It can be the thing that drains us or it can be the thing that challenges and fulfils us. It can be a source of stress or it can be a space where we grow and achieve things we are proud of. I want more people to experience the latter. And that starts with managers – because managers shape the day-to-day reality of work more than anyone else.

So, if you are walking away from this book feeling inspired, that is great. But if you are walking away from it with a plan, if you are already thinking about the next conversation you need to have, the next process you need to refine or the way you want to shift your leadership style, that is even better.

Because the only way to truly step into Your Boss Era is to *live it.*

The difference between good managers and great ones is action. So let's go.

Sources

Part 1: People: Mastering the Mindset

Nancholas, B., 15 Nov. 2024. The importance of soft skills in the workplace. The University of Sunderland. Retrieved from https://online.sunderland.ac.uk/the-importance-of-soft-skills-in-the-workplace.

Rule #1: Own Your Emotions (or They'll Own You)

Carnegie, D., 2006. *How to Win Friends and Influence People*. Vermilion.

Gallup, 2024. State of the global workplace. Retrieved from https://www.gallup.com/workplace/349484/state-of-the-global-workplace.aspx.

Goleman, D., 1995. *Emotional Intelligence: Why it can matter more than IQ*. Bantam.

Goleman, D., 1998. What makes a leader? *Harvard Business Review*, 76(6), pp. 93–102.

TalentSmartEQ, 2023. The latest discoveries on emotional intelligence habits. Retrieved from https://www.talentsmarteq.com/wp-content/uploads/2024/09/TS_EQHabits_ResearchReport_r5.pdf [p. 5].

Rule #3: Leverage the Science of Inspiration and Motivation

Bazigos, M. and Caruso, E., 2 Mar. 2016. Why frontline workers are disengaged. McKinsey & Company.

Retrieved from https://www.mckinsey.com/capabilities/
people-and-organizational-performance/our-insights/
why-frontline-workers-are-disengaged.

Festinger, L., 1 May 1954. A Theory of Social Comparison
Processes. *Human Relations*, 7(2), pp. 117–40.

Gallup, 12 Jan. 2024. The importance of employee recognition:
Low cost, high impact. Retrieved from https://www.gallup.
com/workplace/236441/state-american-manager-report.aspx.

Kiderlin, S., 20 Apr. 2023. Overwhelming majority of Gen
Z workers would quit their jobs over company values,
LinkedIn data says. CNBC. Retrieved from https://www.cnbc.
com/2023/04/20/majority-of-gen-z-would-quit-their-jobs-
over-company-values-linkedin.html.

Lexton, E., 23 Mar. 2023. Engaging your employees is good,
but don't stop there. World Economic Forum. Retrieved
from https://www.weforum.org/stories/2016/03/
engaging-your-employees-is-good-but-don-t-stop-there/.

Xue, H., Luo, Y., Luan, Y. and Wang, N., 2022. A meta-analysis
of leadership and intrinsic motivation: Examining relative
importance and moderators. *Frontiers in Psychology*, 13,
p. 941161.

Rule #4: Embrace the Big Picture: Thinking Strategically

Grant, A., 2016. *Originals: How non-conformists move the world.*
Viking.

Mohammed, S. and Schillinger, D., 10 Nov. 2021. Translating
time-based research into team interventions: An actionable,
evidence-based approach. *Journal of Clinical and Translational
Science*, 6(1), pp. 1–22.

Schwartz, B., 2004. *The Paradox of Choice: Why More Is Less.* ECCO.

TODAY, 5 May 2021. Watch Hoda's Full Interview With Rosalind
Brewer, The Newest CEO of Walgreens. Retrieved from
https://www.youtube.com/watch?v=2t35ETrJygo.

Rule #5: Don't Play the Superhero: Embrace Failure

Bariso, J., 9 Dec. 2019. Jeff Bezos gave an Amazon employee extraordinary advice after his epic fail. It's a lesson in emotional intelligence. Inc. Retrieved from https://www.inc.com/justin-bariso/jeff-bezos-gave-an-amazon-employee-extraordinary-advice-after-his-epic-fail-its-a-lesson-in-emotional-intelligence.html.

Baskin, J., 14 June 2023. Four Steps to Building the Psychological Safety That High-Performing Teams Need. Working Knowledge (Harvard Business School).

Carse, J. P., 1986. *Finite and Infinite Games*. Free Press.

D'Onfro, J., 2 Dec. 2014. Amazon's Jeff Bezos: 'I've Made Billions of Dollars of Failures'. *Entrepeneur*.

Harvard Business Review, 10 May 2022. How to recover from failure. Retrieved from https://store.hbr.org/product/how-to-recover-from-failure-hbr-special-issue/SPSU22?srsltid=AfmBOopFYPcfqqGwwZ-zxpG14ioN-ZTIEMbE1RgHruJwqONlK58rqIHl.

Karpman, S. B., 1 Jan. 1973. 1972 Eric Berne Memorial Scientific Award Lecture. *Transactional Analysis Bulletin*, 3(1), pp. 73–7.

LeaderFactor, 10 Sept. 2024. Project Aristotle: What You Need to Know About Psychological Safety. https://www.youtube.com/watch?v=xLsOjAsUbZo.

Sinek, S. 2019. *The Infinite Game*. Portfolio Penguin.

Rule #6: Choose Respect Over Approval

Covey, S. R., 1989. *The 7 Habits of Highly Effective People: Powerful Lessons in Personal Change*. Free Press.

Rohn, J., 2005. *Twelve Pillars*. Jim Rohn International.

Royal Society for Public Health & Young Health Movement, May 2017. #StatusOfMind: Social media and young people's mental health and wellbeing. RSPH.

Rule #7: Surround Yourself with Great People

Winstanely, G., 21 Feb. 2024. Mentoring Statistics You Need to Know – 2024. Mentorloop.

Rule #8: Show Up as Your Whole Self

Brown, B., 2018. *The Gifts of Imperfection: Let go of who you think you're supposed to be and embrace who you are*. Vermilion.

Burns, U., 2021. *Where You Are Is Not Who You Are*. HarperCollins.

Erskine, J. and Georgiou, G., 2023. Leadership styles: Work stress, related outcomes and health. In: *The Palgrave Handbook of Occupational Stress*. Springer International Publishing, pp. 221–55.

Gavin, M., 3 Mar. 2020. 5 characteristics of a courageous leader. Harvard Business School Online. Retrieved from https://online.hbs.edu/blog/post/courageous-leadership.

Holincheck, J., 27 Oct. 2006. Case Study: Workforce Analytics at Sun. Gartner Research.

Knowledge at Wharton (podcast), 16 May 2007. Workplace Loyalties Change, but the Value of Mentoring Doesn't. Retrieved from https://knowledge.wharton.upenn.edu/podcast/knowledge-at-wharton-podcast/workplace-loyalties-change-but-the-value-of-mentoring-doesnt/.

Sandberg, S., 2015. *Lean In: Women, work, and the will to lead*. WH Allen.

Semedo, A. S., Coelho, A. and Ribeiro, N., 13 May 2019. Authentic leadership, happiness at work and affective commitment: An empirical study in Cape Verde. *European Business Review* 31(3), pp. 337–51.

Wei, F., Li, Y., Zhang, Y. and Liu, S., 2018. The interactive effect of authentic leadership and leader competency on followers' job performance: The mediating role of work engagement. *Journal of Business Ethics*, 153(3), pp. 763–73.

Wells, J. E. and MacAulay, D., 12 Aug. 2024. Invisible mending: The silent struggle of conforming at work. *Psychology Today*. Retrieved from https://www. psychologytoday.com/gb/blog/our-invisible-work/202408/ invisible-mending-the-silent-struggle-of-conforming-at-work.

Rule #9: Don't Improve Your Weaknesses, Play to Your Strengths

Csikszentmihalyi, M., 2008. *Flow: The psychology of optimal experience*. HarperCollins.

Gallup, n.d. Strengths development & coaching. Retrieved from https://www.gallup.com/learning/248405/strengths-development-coaching.aspx.

Laoyan, S., 5 Mar. 2024. Understanding the Pareto Principle (The 80/20 Rule). Asana. Retrieved from https://asana.com/ resources/pareto-principle-80-20-rule.

Schatz, J., 17 Jul. 2022. 5 ways to increase employee engagement. Gallup. Retrieved from https://www.gallup.com/workplace/ 231581/five-ways-improve-employee-engagement.aspx.

Vohs, K., Baumeister, R. and Twenge, J., Jan. 2005. Decision Fatigue Exhausts Self-Regulatory Resources – But So Does Accommodating to Unchosen Alternatives. *Psychology Today*. Retrieved from: https://cdn2.psychologytoday.com/assets/ attachments/584/decision200602-15vohs.pdf.

Rule #10: Get to Know Your Team (the 1-on-1 System)

Kochhar, R., 1 Mar. 2023. The Enduring Grip of the Gender Pay Gap. Pew Research Center. Retrieved from https:// www.pewresearch.org/social-trends/2023/03/01/ the-enduring-grip-of-the-gender-pay-gap/.

McLain, D. and Nelson, B., 1 Jan. 2022. How effective feedback fuels performance. Gallup. Retrieved from https://www.

gallup.com/workplace/357764/fast-feedback-fuels-
performance.aspx.

SKYbrary. Authority Gradients. Retrieved from https://skybrary.
aero/articles/authority-gradients.

Rule #11: Have the Courage to Confront

Ferriss, T., 2007. *The 4-Hour Work Week: Escape the 9–5, live
anywhere, and join the new rich.* Crown Publishing Group.

Rule #12: Stop Making Decisions

Columbia Business School, 14 Apr. 2011. A judge's willingness
to grant parole can be influenced by breaks. ScienceDaily.
Retrieved from https://www.sciencedaily.com/
releases/2011/04/110413151639.htm.

Hastings, R. and Meyer, E., 2024. *No Rules Rules: Netflix and the
culture of reinvention.* WH Allen.

Kahneman, D. and Tversky, A., Mar. 1979. Prospect Theory:
An Analysis of Decision under Risk. *Econometrica*, 47(2), pp.
263–92.

Langer, E. J., 1975. The illusion of control. *Journal of Personality and
Social Psychology*, 32(2), p. 311.

Rule #13: Talk Like the Boss

Gallup, 12 Jan. 2024. The importance of employee recognition:
Low cost, high impact. Retrieved from https://www.gallup.
com/workplace/236441/state-american-manager-report.aspx.

Emerson, R. M., Aug. 1976. Social Exchange Theory. *Annual
Review of Sociology*, 2, pp. 335–62.

MacArthur, H. V., 12 Feb. 2025. The power of listening: Building
bridges and fostering collaboration. *Forbes*. Retrieved from
https://www.forbes.com/sites/hvmacarthur/2025/02/01/

the-power-of-listening-building-bridges-and-fostering-collaboration/.

Nickerson, C., 25 Oct. 2023. Social Exchange Theory of Relationships: Examples & More. Simply Psychology. Retrieved from https://www.simplypsychology.org/what-is-social-exchange-theory.html.

The Diary Of A CEO, 20 Jan. 2025. The Money Making Expert (NEW): The 7,11,4 Hack That Turns $1 Into $10K Per Month! Daniel Priestley. https://www.youtube.com/watch?v=sFkR34AMPw8.

Rule #14: Understand KPIs (and Empower Your Team to Actually Hit Them)

Bas, A. A History of Objectives and Key Results (OKRs). Peoplelogic. Retrieved from https://peoplelogic.ai/blog/history-of-objectives-and-key-results.

Darley, J. M. and Latané, B., 1968. Bystander intervention in emergencies: Diffusion of responsibility. *Journal of Personality and Social Psychology*, 8, pp. 377–83.

Grimpe, C. and Kaiser, U., 2010. Balancing internal and external knowledge acquisition: The gains and pains from R&D outsourcing. *Journal of Management Studies*, 47(8), pp. 1483–509.

Hastings, R. and Meyer, E., 2024. *No Rules Rules: Netflix and the culture of reinvention*. WH Allen.

Life Stories, 29 Aug. 2023. Sheryl Sandberg Interview: From Google to Facebook. https://www.youtube.com/watch?v=mxiTTRbilsk.

Smith, M., 2023. 2022–2023 SHRM State of the Workplace Report. SHRM. Retrieved from https://www.shrm.org/content/dam/en/shrm/research/2022-2023-State-of-the-Workplace-Report.pdf.

Rule #15: Use Accountability to Turn Goals into Action

Culture Partners, 14 Sep. 2019. Landmark workplace study reveals crisis of accountability. Retrieved from https://culturepartners.com/insights/landmark-workplace-study-reveals-crisis-of-accountability/.

Ferguson, A., 2016. *Leading: Learning from life and my years at Manchester United.* Grand Central Publishing.

Gallup. Re-Engineering Performance Management. Retrieved from https://www.gallup.com/workplace/238064/re-engineering-performance-management.aspx.

Guggenberger, P., Maor, D., Park, M. and Simon, P., 26 Apr. 2023. The State of Organizations 2023: Ten shifts transforming organizations. McKinsey & Company. Retrieved from https://www.mckinsey.org/capabilities/people-and-organizational-performance/our-insights/the-state-of-organizations-2023.

Lockwood Primus, K., 14 Sept. 2023. Are You Holding Yourself and Your Team Accountable in the Right Way? *Forbes.* Retrieved from https://www.forbes.com/councils/forbeshumanresourcescouncil/2023/09/14/are-you-holding-yourself-and-your-team-accountable-in-the-right-way/.

Rule #16: Focus on What Matters

Asana, 2023. The Anatomy of Work Global Index. Retrieved from https://asana.com/resources/anatomy-of-work.

Talbert, M., 12 Feb. 2025. The way we work isn't working. Asana. Retrieved from https://asana.com/resources/work-isnt-working.

Acknowledgements

Writing a book is never a solo act. It's a collection of encouragements, challenges, and unseen moments that others have poured into you, and I have many people to thank.

To my two incredible leadership coaches in 2020–2023, Cheryl Thompson and Marianne Page, thank you for shaping not just my leadership, but who I am. Cheryl, your strength as a feminist, activist, and mentor taught me how to believe in myself when I so often handed away the credit for my success to others. You helped me see my own power, and I will carry those lessons with me for the rest of my life. Marianne, you gave me the priceless gift of clarity through systemisation and operations – showing me that building something strong and lasting isn't about doing more, but doing better. Your wisdom changed the way I think about leadership and business forever.

To my editor, Géraldine, thank you for taking a chance on this project, treating it with such care, and always giving me the blunt honesty I didn't always want but definitely needed. Your sharp eye, high standards, and belief in this book made it infinitely better.

To the Fresh Leadership World community – this book wouldn't exist without you. Your willingness to share your struggles, your deepest thoughts, your fears and hopes, has shaped not just these pages, but me as a person. Every message you've sent, every story you've trusted me with, every vulnerable moment you've shared – it all became the true heartbeat behind this book. Thank you for letting me walk alongside you on your leadership journeys. I hope this book feels like the conversation we've been having all along.

To my two grandmothers and my mum – the three women who shaped my life in ways too big to measure. Times weren't as easy for you as they were for me. To Granny Aud, who raised four kids as a single mum in a council house, but still somehow filling every day with a crazy, unshakeable positivity. Grandma Elaine, for showing me the power of perseverance – taking yourself to night school whilst Grandad was down the pit, with two young children by your side, even when it was frowned upon for women to work back then, and passed on your deep love of books that shaped my imagination from the very start. Mum, to building a business with nothing but grit and belief, you showed me what strength really looks like. You taught me that resilience, ambition, and hope can live side by side – and because of you, I knew it was possible to dream bigger. This book, this life, all of it has your fingerprints all over it.

And finally, to my wonderful fiancée, Charlotte – thank you for believing in me when I couldn't always see the path forward. For every late-night teary conversation, every moment you sat with me through the doubts, the second-guessing, the 'can I really do this?' moments, you were always my anchor. Your patience, your love, and your quiet, unwavering faith in me kept me going when it would have been so easy to stop. This book is as much yours as it is mine.

Thank you, from the bottom of my heart.